IN UTER

Praise for the

It was only a matter of time before a clever publisher realized that there is an audience for whom *Exile on Main Street* or *Electric Ladyland* are as significant and worthy of study as *The Catcher in the Rye* or *Middlemarch* ... The series ... is freewheeling and eclectic, ranging from minute rock-geek analysis to idiosyncratic personal celebration — *The New York Times Book Review*

Ideal for the rock geek who thinks liner notes just aren't enough — *Rolling Stone*

One of the coolest publishing imprints on the planet — *Bookslut*

These are for the insane collectors out there who appreciate fantastic design, well-executed thinking, and things that make your house look cool. Each volume in this series takes a seminal album and breaks it down in startling minutiae. We love these. We are huge nerds — *Vice*

A brilliant series ... each one a work of real love — *NME* (UK)

Passionate, obsessive, and smart — *Nylon*

Religious tracts for the rock 'n' roll faithful — *Boldtype*

[A] consistently excellent series — *Uncut* (UK)

We ... aren't naive enough to think that we're your only source for reading about music (but if we had our way ... watch out). For those of you who really like to know everything there is to know about an album, you'd do well to check out Continuum's "33 1/3" series of books — *Pitchfork*

For reviews of individual titles in the series, please visit our blog at 333sound.com and our website at http://www.bloomsbury.com/musicandsoundstudies

Follow us on Twitter: @333books

Like us on Facebook: https://www.facebook.com/33.3books

For a complete list of books in this series, see the back of this book

For more information about the series, please visit our new blog:

www.333sound.com

Where you'll find:

– Author and artist interviews

– Author profiles

– News about the series

– How to submit a proposal to our open call

– Things we find amusing

In Utero

Gillian G. Gaar

BLOOMSBURY ACADEMIC
NEW YORK • LONDON • OXFORD • NEW DELHI • SYDNEY

BLOOMSBURY ACADEMIC
Bloomsbury Publishing Inc
1385 Broadway, New York, NY 10018, USA
50 Bedford Square, London, WC1B 3DP, UK
29 Earlsfort Terrace, Dublin 2, Ireland

BLOOMSBURY, BLOOMSBURY ACADEMIC and the Diana logo are
trademarks of Bloomsbury Publishing Plc

First published in Great Britain 2006 by the Continuum International
Publishing Group Inc
Reprinted 2012
Reprinted by Bloomsbury Academic 2013, 2014 (twice), 2015, 2016, 2018,
2019, 2020, 2022 (twice), 2023, 2024

Bloomsbury Publishing Inc does not have any control over, or responsibility
for, any third-party websites referred to or in this book. All internet addresses
given in this book were correct at the time of going to press. The author and
publisher regret any inconvenience caused if addresses have changed or sites
have ceased to exist, but can accept no responsibility for any such changes.

Library of Congress Cataloging-in-Publication Data
Gaar, Gillian G., 1959-
In utero/Gillian G. Gaar.
p. cm. – (33 1/3)
Includes bibliographical references.
ISBN-13: 978-0-8264-1776-3 (pbk.: alk. paper)
ISBN-10: 0-8264-1776-0 (pbk.: alk. paper)
1. Nirvana (Musical group). In utero. 2. Nirvana (Musical group)
I. Title.
II. Series.
ML421.N57G33 2006
782.42166092'2–dc22
200601604

ISBN: PB: 978-0-8264-1776-3
ePDF: 978-1-4411-8609-6
eBook: 978-1-4411-9364-3

Series: 33 1/3, volume 34

Printed and bound in Great Britain

To find out more about our authors and books visit www.bloomsbury.com
and sign up for our newsletters.

Acknowledgments

Thanks to David Barker for commissioning this book.
Thanks to all my interviewees over the years: Steve
Albini, Bill Arnold, Earnie Bailey, Anton Corbijn, Jack
Endino, Robert Fisher, Craig Montgomery, Krist
Novoselic, Charles Peterson, all of whom answered
repeated inquiries. Special thanks to my transcriptionists,
especially Carrie Stamper and Natalie Walker; also Katie
Hansen, Nick Tamburro, Julia Voss. Thanks to Dr. Chris
Belcher and Carol Nicholson for keeping my hands and
arms working. Thanks to Carrie Borzillo-Vrenna, Kris
Sproul, Alex Roberts, Mike Ziegler, and mom, for servic-
es rendered. And of course, thanks to Nirvana, for all
their music.

To Jack Endino
for wanting to dig into the details as much as I do

Chapter 1
Life on the Verge

As 1993 began, it was the best of times and the worst of times for Nirvana.

On the plus side, in the fall of 1991 they'd vaulted seemingly overnight (in reality, the result of five years' hard work) from near obscurity to global domination. Their second album, 1991's *Nevermind*, wasn't just a breakthrough for the band, it was a high watermark for the entire alternative rock scene. Indeed, when *Nevermind* supplanted Michael Jackson's *Dangerous* at the top of the *Billboard* record charts in January 1992 it symbolized a changing of the musical guard as the very term "alternative rock" finally entered the mainstream lexicon, a genre quickly divided into "pre-Nirvana" and "post-Nirvana" markets.

But ironically, the band's very success also threatened to implode the trio, comprised of lead guitarist, singer, and primary songwriter Kurt Cobain, bassist Krist Novoselic, and drummer Dave Grohl. Though denied at the time, Cobain's escalating heroin use had severely curtailed the band's touring schedule, and when they did tour, shows were occasionally cancelled due to "illness" (in 1991 the band played 88 shows; in 1992, they played 35). Cobain entered various detox programs during the year, but when an article in the September 1992 issue of *Vanity Fair* claimed Cobain's wife, Courtney Love, used heroin while pregnant (a charge she has always denied), the couple temporarily lost custody of their daughter, Frances Bean Cobain, born August 18. A dispute over songwriting royalties nearly split the group in the spring. They were even sued over their name by two members of a 1960s-era British group also called Nirvana (a case eventually settled out of court for $100,000).

But by the end of '92, things had somewhat stabilized in the Nirvana camp. Defying rumors of their break-up, the band headlined England's Reading Festival on August 30, widely considered one of their best performances. At the end of October, they entered a recording studio for the first time in nearly seven months to begin work on *Nevermind*'s follow-up. Within another year, that album, *In Utero*, would be recorded, released, and again hit the top of the *Billboard* charts.

Yet, while far from being the unlistenable career-killer the press speculated it might be, a deliberate attempt on the part of the band to alienate their newfound audience, *In Utero* did serve as something of, in Novoselic's words, "a litmus test towards our audience...in terms of mainstream appeal, it won't have the glossiness of *Nevermind*." *In Utero* was anything but glossy, but by this point in their career the band's musicianship was of such high caliber they could hardly drop back to the sludginess of their first album, 1989's *Bleach*. *In Utero* was also more highly anticipated than either of those records had been, arguably the most eagerly awaited rock record of 1993, and one that was sure to be scrutinized for any clue to the band's—particularly Cobain's—inner psyche. Still, despite the pressure—from their audience, from their label and management, and themselves—Nirvana admirably rose to the challenge. Though *In Utero* would never approach the sales success of *Nevermind*—nor did the band expect, or care, that it would —it was nonetheless an album of remarkable depth, with startling lyrical imagery and music that ranged from abrasive punk to richly textured pop, an assured and mature work that was largely the creation of a man who turned 26 as the album was being recorded.

Yet the album also had a surprisingly long gestation. Songs that would eventually be recorded during the *In Utero* sessions in February 1993 were first attempted as far back as 1990. The record would also be the source of several controversies, from the sound of its production, to the album artwork and song titles, to the conception of the album's sole video. And after Cobain's suicide in April 1994, just over six months after *In Utero*'s release, it would be examined even more closely for clues of his impending demise.

In the end, of course, it's the music that matters, and while *Nevermind* has secured the commercial kudos, increasingly over the years it's *In Utero* that's cited as the group's artistically strongest album. And given that the album was both born of and a reaction to Nirvana's extraordinary success, the highly charged atmosphere surrounding the creation of *In Utero* is as much a part of the story as the music itself.

Chapter 2
The Saga of "Sappy"

One song recorded at the *In Utero* sessions has perhaps the most curious history of any number in Nirvana's catalogue; the song originally entitled "Sappy." Over the course of three and a half years, it would be recorded four times, with three different producers (including Steve Albini, *In Utero*'s producer), and two different drummers. It was the *In Utero* version that would ultimately be released, but even then it was almost sneaked out the door, appearing as an uncredited, "secret" track on a charity compilation.

The earliest known version of the song appears on a home demo with Cobain accompanying himself on guitar, recorded in the late 80s. This version is the most mournful, with a lyric droning about the ways of achieving happiness, that Cobain sings almost sonambulistically (though not officially released, this version has been bootlegged). The band added it to their live set on their first European tour in the fall of 1989, and on January 2 and 3, 1990, recorded the first studio version of the song at Seattle's Reciprocal Recording with producer Jack Endino (though on Nirvana's records, Endino eschewed the "Producer" credit, preferring it read "Recorded By").

The band had previously worked with Endino on their very first studio session, when they recorded a ten-track demo with drummer Dale Crover, and later sessions for the "Love Buzz" single and *Bleach* album. During the "Sappy" session (with Chad Channing now on drums), a total of ten hours were spent in the studio (seven hours the first day, three hours the next), at that point the longest time the band had spent working on a single song. "They ended up wasting a tremendous amount of time," Endino recalls, much of that spent trying to nail down the right drum sound. "They literally wanted an Albini drum sound," says Endino. "They wanted a lot of room mics, and, frankly, the room at Reciprocal was a lousy room to put room mics in; it was a very dead-sounding room. I did the best I could, and it actually sounds pretty Albini-esque, if I dare say so myself! We spent a lot of time experimenting with reverbs and gated room mics and just doing lots of strange stuff during the mix. Kurt was definitely looking to try some different stuff; he had very specific ideas for how he wanted the drums to sound and how he wanted the vocals to sound. That's why it took so long."

This version would have the most "rock" feel of the

early studio versions, with a fuzzier guitar sound and a higher pitched vocal. The song was also tightened up, eliminating the opening bars of instrumental introduction. The lyric was also somewhat different, though the refrain about being in a laundry room was common to all versions. This was also the first version to feature an instrumental bridge, which included a guitar solo from Cobain. But it remained unreleased until its inclusion on *Sliver: The Best of the Box* in 2005.

Three months later, when the group arrived at Smart Studios in Madison, Wisconsin, to work on what they assumed would be their second album for Sub Pop, they recorded "Sappy" a second time (the sessions running from April 2 to 6, 1990). It marked the first time Nirvana worked with producer Butch Vig. Though recorded with the full band, this version has more of the acoustic feel of the original demo, with both Channing's drum work and Cobain's solo being more restrained; it also features a four-bar instrumental intro before the vocal begins. This version remains unreleased, though it has been extensively bootlegged.

Over the next year, much changed for Nirvana. Channing left the group, replaced by Dave Grohl on drums. The band signed a management contract with the Gold Mountain agency (who also looked after Sonic Youth, a band Nirvana much admired and had opened for), signed a major label record contract with DGC, a subsidiary of Geffen (and also Sonic Youth's label), and, on May 2, 1991, entered Sound City Recording Studios in Van Nuys, California, to record their major label debut.

Eight months later, the album the group recorded at Sound City, *Nevermind*, would top the US charts. Cobain would be hailed the new spokesman of his generation, and *Nevermind*'s lyrics would be critiqued and analyzed extensively. But there were another three songs recorded during the sessions that were not released on the album; "Old Age" and "Verse Chorus Verse" (both of which appeared on the 2004 box set *With the Lights Out*), and yet another version of "Sappy."

"Obviously, there was something that didn't work on the previous version and Kurt wanted to try and do it again," says Vig, who also produced the *Nevermind* sessions. "Maybe Kurt in his head thought it would gel into something that was amazing. Maybe he thought if they tried it again that one day everything would fall into place. Maybe he didn't want to give up. Sometimes you get a song and you record it one way and you go, 'The song just didn't happen.' Then you try it again. But after three tries, you've gotta give up. You have to realize the song is not meant to happen. But maybe Kurt heard something that we didn't hear, and that's what he was trying to get, and he never got it. Sometimes that happens; you get these mental images of a song, and you know it's going to be good, but if it gets to a certain point and it never gets there, it kind of drives you crazy."

This version was in a different key to the previous versions, and featured a few lyrical changes; the guitar solo, though similar to the previous version recorded with Vig, was also subtly different and decidedly more confident. The song also began without the instrumental opening. But the band abandoned further work on it, leaving this version of the song in the realm of parlor-game pondering; had it been used on *Nevermind*, what track on the album should it have replaced? Cobain himself reworked his second record's lineup a number of times, as seen in his *Journals*, with various track listings putting "Sappy" in the running. Little of the material in *Journals* is dated, but the lists were presumably made before the spring of 1991, when landmark *Nevermind* tracks like "Smells Like Teen Spirit" and "Come As You Are" were written; once those songs appear on Cobain's potential track listings "Sappy" drops off.

But neither could Cobain leave the song alone; nearly two years after the *Nevermind* sessions, the band would again record the song with Albini. "Something just drove Kurt to keep busting it out," says Krist Novoselic. "Maybe he thought he was going to put that song over the top. He had some kind of unattainable expectations for it, I don't know. We all just played it the same way. I really liked the way I played bass on it, so I never changed it. Maybe he just thought we were going to get the right performance or something," The final live performance of the song would be on February 25 at the Palatrussardi in Milan, Italy, less than six weeks before Cobain's death.

Chapter 3
The Music Source Session

"They just had some ideas they wanted to throw down," is how Craig Montgomery recalls his first recording session with Nirvana on January 1, 1991 at the Music Source studio in Seattle, where the group had previously recorded five tracks with producer Steve Fisk in September 1989 (with Channing on drums). "I had been bugging them to let me record them," Montgomery continues. "And I had a friend who worked at the Music Source and he said he could get us in there for free. I was young and naïve and I thought that if the session went really great they might let me work on their next record."

Montgomery had been the band's sound tech since Nirvana's first European tour in the fall of 1989. By the time of the January 1991 session, the band had signed their management contract with Gold Mountain and were preparing to sign with DGC. But as their contract would not be signed until April 30, 1991, and they had no further commitments to their current label, Sub Pop, this session seems to have functioned as something of a rehearsal for the group, and, given that it was their first recording session with drummer Grohl, a chance to see how the band would work together in the studio. The previous night, the band had played a show in Portland, Oregon, then drove up to Seattle, and though Montgomery recalls their gear as being "all beat up," the group themselves "were in pretty good shape. They were ready to work. They were pretty efficient by Nirvana standards."

Most of the seven tracks recorded, aside from "Token Eastern Song" (which had been previously recorded with Fisk and was a part of the band's live set but was never performed again after this session) later appeared in some form: "Aneurysm" and "Even in His Youth" (the latter also previously recorded with Fisk) were released later that year on the "Smells Like Teen Spirit" CD single, "On a Plain" was re-recorded for *Nevermind*, and "Oh, the Guilt" was re-recorded and released as a split single with the Jesus Lizard in 1993. And two of the songs were later re-recorded for *In Utero*: "Radio Friendly Unit Shifter" and "All Apologies."

"Radio Friendly" (untitled at the time) was a new song that had come together during the band's jam sessions. The song is believed to have been played only once before, at a show at Seattle's Off Ramp club on November 25, 1990, and a 29-second clip of the song said to be from the show surfaced on the internet in 2002. Wherever the clip is from, the musical structure is similar to the final version, while the lyrics are completely different; the version recorded with Montgomery has a barely audible scratch vocal, and so for all practical purposes can be considered an instrumental.

Even at this early stage, the musical backing was fully worked out; a single, driving riff playing through the entire song save for an instrumental bridge. But what might have become monotonous in another band's hands is here surprisingly compelling, for the music captures Nirvana at their power-trio best; simply guitar, bass, and drums coalescing into a powerful whole. The strength of Grohl's drumming also makes it clear what his attraction was to Cobain and Novoselic; only Dale Crover had hit the drums as hard. "Dave was a breath of fresh air," says Montgomery. "He could play solid and steady and could sing and was fun to be around."

Conversely, "All Apologies" had been around since 1990, and the band would start to perform it on their fall 1991 tour. The Music Source version was markedly different in its musical feel to the later released version, having a more upbeat pop-folk sound, with Cobain playing the song's hypnotic main riff accompanied by Novoselic also on guitar instead of bass; "Krist was playing these 7th chords that give the whole thing a different feel than it later had," Montgomery says. Having the drum beats accented by flourishes of tambourine gave the song an additional lighthearted flavor, akin to the pop spirits of "Sliver."

But as usual, though the musical arrangement was largely worked out, the words were far from being finalized, and would be changed substantially for the final version. An undated demo of "All Apologies" appears on the box set *With the Lights Out*, with Cobain accompanying himself on acoustic guitar; the lyrics are closer to the released version, suggesting the demo was recorded after this 1991 session. "It's obviously well known that lyrics for Kurt always came last, sometimes not even until it was time to record the real thing," says Montgomery. "I think that might have been a source of some anxiety or stress for him. It's like being in school and having to have your homework done. It's not that he had a shortage of words to draw from, because he was always writing things down. But writing lyrics for songs is hard. It's not easy." Books like *Journals* and Michael Azerrad's authorized Nirvana biography *Come As You Are* both reprint drafts of Cobain's lyrics, showing how much he tinkered with them before recording the final version.

Aside from the occasional instrumental overdub, "the session was pretty quick and dirty," says Montgomery. "To set up, get sounds, play a bunch of songs, and do some kind of a mix in one day is obviously really quick and dirty. So my thinking during the session wasn't really song oriented, it was more technical. The vocals are all scratch vocals; we didn't redo any vocal tracks, it's all just Kurt screaming in the room along with the drums and guitars into a not real nice vocal mic. This was just a day of goofing around, basically. I was just hoping to show them what I could do in the studio. It's hard to break into recording, and to be able to sit there in the studio and have a band like Nirvana as your guinea pig is a huge opportunity. I was learning as I went and so were they—we all were." As for the music itself, Montgomery says "There were some songs in here that I really liked, thinking, 'Wow, this is a great song, they could really do something with this.'" They soon would.

Chapter 4
The Word of Mouth Sessions

"We're going into the studio as soon as we get back to Seattle," Cobain told journalist Everett True on June 30, 1992, discussing Nirvana's upcoming album. "What I'd like to do is to go to Reciprocal with Jack Endino…record the songs with Jack on an eight track, record them somewhere else on a 24 track with Steve Albini, and then pick the best." And though neither producer had been contacted at that point, what Cobain had outlined would in fact happen. Nirvana wouldn't step into a studio for another four months, but when they did it was indeed Reciprocal Recording, by that time rechristened Word of Mouth. And they were once again working with Jack Endino.

Nirvana's only other studio sessions in 1992 were in April at the Laundry Room, then located in West Seattle and run by Barrett Jones, a friend of Grohl's from Virginia. On April 7, 1992, Nirvana recorded three songs at the Laundry

Room, "Curmudgeon" and "Oh, the Guilt," which ended up on singles, and "Return of the Rat," which appeared on a Wipers tribute album. On another date that month they recorded an instrumental version of "Frances Farmer Will Have Her Revenge on Seattle." Though slower than the final version, this early take shows that the musical arrangement was already in place.

The recordings laid down October 25-26, 1992 at Word of Mouth would, with one exception, be instrumentals. Endino had not worked in the studio with the group since July 1990, when Nirvana recorded "Sliver" at Reciprocal, and he was immediately struck by high degree of tension among the members. "The atmosphere was strained," Endino recalls. "Everything was very strained. There was no communication going on between them at all; they were barely even speaking to each other. They didn't waste any time when I was working with them before; that was why this was such a shock—everything was completely different at that session. I have said this many times—what I was seeing now was a completely dysfunctional band that wasn't even talking to each other." Adding to the tension on the first day was that Kurt arrived several hours late. "I remember asking, 'Is this normal? Why is he so late?'" says Endino. "And whoever it was just shrugging and going, 'You get used to this when you're dealing with Kurt.' But once they got playing, they played really hard and went through the songs really fast."

Recording finally started on October 26. The sessions began with three takes of "Dumb," all instrumental, though the song had been performed live since 1990. For all that Cobain would deride the traditional "verse-chorus-verse" song structure, "Dumb" followed the formula to the letter: verse, chorus, verse, chorus, the bridge, verse, chorus, verse, and a final four bars of closing. The performances are restrained; the song was one of the few Nirvana songs that's low-key from beginning to end (similar to "About a Girl" from *Bleach*).

Almost as if needing to blow off steam, the group then recorded an improvisational jam, similar to the kinds of squalling noise-fests they'd play during rehearsals. Endino has always had a fondness for this jam; "I think it's awesome!" he says. "It's like four minutes of just guitar attack. And there's none of that stuff on any of their records; you never get to hear them just jamming like that." An excerpt of the jam was featured on one of the menus on *With the Lights Out*'s DVD.

Afterward, it was back to work, with three instrumental takes of "Frances Farmer Will Have Her Revenge on Seattle." Without the lyrics, it's even easier to hear the band's trademark soft/loud dynamic—the Nirvana "formula"—at work, with the verses starting quietly, swelling at the end of each line, finally exploding with full force in the chorus. In between the second and third take of the song, the band also recorded "tourette's," a song they'd debuted at the

Reading Festival two months earlier. The song is a more structured version of the jam they'd played earlier in the session, with a pile-driving riff played repeatedly throughout, broken up by sudden stops as if needing to catch a breath before diving back in. Though Cobain had screamed out indecipherable lyrics at Reading, this version remained instrumental.

The two takes of "Pennyroyal Tea" were also instrumental, though the song had been written at the time *Nevermind* was recorded and had been performed since 1991, with lyrics in varying stages of completion. But the musical arrangement had evidently been worked out to the group's satisfaction, for it's the same one that would be used on *In Utero*.

The first take of "Rape Me" was also instrumental. The song was first performed in 1991, though at that point lyrics for the bridge had not been written. The song had been at the center of heated discussions the previous month, when Nirvana had wanted to play it at the MTV Video Music Awards ceremony on September 9. MTV executives were not pleased that the band not only didn't want to play one of their hit singles, they wanted to play a song with controversial sounding lyrics. The band only backed down when informed that a friend of theirs working at the network would be fired if they played the song. Nonetheless, Cobain couldn't resist thumbing his nose at MTV, playing the opening bars of the song before launching into "Lithium."

The second take did feature vocals by Cobain, backing vocals by Grohl, and another, more disturbing element; the wails of Cobain's daughter, Frances Bean Cobain. On the second day of the session, Courtney had arrived with Frances in tow, and Kurt held her on his lap as he cut his vocal. "The song is supposed to be very much of a finger pointing song," says Endino, "and to have a little baby there, it's like—'Come on, I'm innocent.' What could be more jarring than the juxtaposition of someone singing 'Rape me!' and having a little baby crying?" Certainly Frances' cries added a disquieting subtext to the already incendiary subject matter—as Nirvana's fans would hear for themselves when this version of the song was released on *With the Lights Out*. The box set also has a home demo of "Rape Me" said to be from 1992, though the lyrics are quite different from those Cobain had already performed in concert.

The last song recorded at the session was an instrumental take of "Radio Friendly Unit Shifter." It's a heavier, rawer version than the one previously recorded with Montgomery, with more squalling guitar noises from Cobain and Grohl's drumming being especially fierce—strong enough, in fact, to draw the attention of the authorities. "Since 1986, we'd had one noise complaint, which was when I was recording Vexed," Endino says. "But once Dave Grohl was in there playing his drums, he was apparently louder than everyone else who had recorded in the past five years, and the cops showed up and asked me to turn it down. And I said, 'You know, I got Nirvana in there, they're this huge band.' But this cop said, 'I don't care who you got in there, you gotta turn it down.'" With that, the session came to an end.

Aware that the band was preparing to record their third album, but unhappy at how strained the sessions had been, Endino had mixed feelings about working with Nirvana again. "During the sessions, all they did was talk about Albini," Endino recalls. "Kurt was like, 'What do you think, do you think we should have Albini do the record?' And what am I going to say? 'No. You should have me do the record.' I just kept my mouth shut. It was obvious the record company was going to want *Nevermind* Version 2, and the band was very obviously not going to make that. I mean, they said to everyone who would listen that they wanted to make a really aggressive punk rock album. So whoever ended up being the producer was going to be between a rock and a hard place; he's either going to have to be a total asshole with the band, in which case they would totally hate him, or he does what the band wants and has the total weight of the record company coming down on his head. And probably the only person in the world who could withstand that was Albini; he can actually do what he wants and stand up to the record company and say no. I'm afraid I would have just chickened out on it. I frankly was sort of like well, if they ask me to do it I will do it, but if they don't ask me I won't complain."

Endino did ask if the band wanted to return later to

record vocals. "And Kurt was like, 'Oh we'll call and let you know,'" he says. "But no one ever set up another session to finish it. And no one ever called for the tapes. They just couldn't be bothered really. I got the feeling that someone had made them come and do the demo just to do a demo, that it wasn't really their idea. I didn't ask them that explicitly, but they didn't seem all too interested." Nonetheless, it's worth pointing out that aside from the jam, Nirvana recorded versions of all these songs for *In Utero.*

The master tape boxes were inscribed "S. Ritchie" on the sides, at the band's request, both as an in-joke (taken from the real name of Sex Pistols bassist Sid Vicious—John Simon Ritchie) and as a way of deflecting attention from people who might take notice of a box marked "Nirvana" in the studio's storage area. When the studio closed the following year, Endino took the boxes home with him, "just waiting for someone to tell me what to do with them. I never told anyone I had them." He kept them until 1998, when work began on *With the Lights Out* and he handed them over to Novoselic.

Chapter 5
The Brazil Sessions

In January 1993, Nirvana flew to Brazil to perform two shows, at São Paulo on the 16th and Rio de Janeiro on the 23rd. While in Rio de Janeiro, the group went into BMG Ariola Studios January 19-21 and recorded further demos. "It was BMG's fancy studio in Rio, but this was their B room," says Craig Montgomery. "It was actually much cooler than their A room because it had an old Neve board and a great old Studer tape deck; it was a really nice room. But the stuff was old—it took awhile to figure out how to get the headphone mixes to work. So that was a little bit frustrating. You don't keep the world's biggest rock band waiting while you try to get the headphones working—you have that stuff working before they get there. But once we got it all working it was a nice recording environment."

"We just had time off so we used the studio," Novoselic recalls of the session. "We were just screwing around, trying some songs out, trying some bass lines and riffs." Of the nine songs recorded, six would later be re-recorded, and four of those would appear on *In Utero*. All the songs were in a more complete state, compared to the previous session at Word of Mouth; even the improvisational numbers had lyrics. The songs were also new, and most had yet to be performed live.

The songs were mostly recorded live, with little overdubbing. "We didn't redo any vocals," says Montgomery. "Kurt, he wanted to get out of there. He was the last one in there and the first to leave all week. The sounds are also more direct. Albini is really into recording rooms and recording things from across the room and hearing how it bounces off the walls. Sometimes you get so busy recording rooms that it doesn't sound very musical to me. I'm more into hearing a song than a room, and you can quote me on that. There was also a great big cabinet of really nice microphones, and I took advantage of that. I had really nice mics on everything. And we spent some time on the guitar sounds. Besides the microphone on the amp, I also took a direct feed, which is why you have that really direct and dirty sound. Kurt was into that too, he wanted that direct intothe-board distortion kind of sound. And by this time I had done a few more records for other people, so I knew what I was doing more."

The most notable song recorded at the session, which would also be one of the highlights of *In Utero*, was also the first song recorded, "Heart-Shaped Box." Montgomery remembers first hearing the song at the band's soundcheck in São Paulo. "Even then Kurt knew this was the single," he says. "This was the formula for a single. All the other stuff they had was way more noisy and abrasive than this. Even the other sound guys that were out there on the platform with me were going, 'Yeah, this is a good song.' I don't know if it was a conscious effort on his part to write the new single, but that was the vibe it had." Earnie Bailey, the band's guitar tech who was also in Brazil, was equally impressed. "You could tell that this was an important song in a lot of ways," he says. "You knew that it just had a lot of weight to it, even the first time you heard it."

The song was ostensibly a love song directed toward Cobain's wife, though, like "About a Girl," which had been about a previous girlfriend, it had a decidedly bitter undercurrent. Bailey recalls an earlier title of the song being "New Complaint," and the "box" in the title and lyric had originally been a coffin. There was an initial take of the song to test the studio equipment, then a second take was recorded. As usual, the lyrics hadn't been fully worked out and Cobain essentially repeats variations of the first verse three times. The instrumental break also has a far more experimental solo, more akin to the group's improvs. "I'm biased, but except for the fact that it doesn't have a finished vocal, I actually like the sound of this better than the one on *In Utero*," says Montgomery. This version of the song later appeared on *With the Lights Out*.

With the Lights Out also provided an exciting opportunity to hear a Nirvana song in the process of coming together, as over the course of nine minutes you can hear "Scentless Apprentice" evolving from its opening riff into something approximating a full-fledged song at one of the band's rehearsals. "Some songs just came out of nowhere," says Novoselic. "Dave had that riff from 'Scentless Apprentice.' That pretty much just came out of a jam. And then I threw in that other riff after that. And then it all came together, man!" Cobain told Michael Azerrad he'd initially been reluctant to work with Grohl's idea, as he'd found it "such a cliché grunge Tad riff." "But I just decided to write a song with that just to make him feel better," he said, "and it turned out really cool." In this first rehearsal, the main riff is pounded out and Cobain's guitar goes off on different experimental tangents until hitting a riff that spirals upward; the two riffs lock together and provide the energetic base of the song.

The "Scentless Apprentice" recorded in Brazil was closer to its final running time on *In Utero*, though Cobain makes no attempt to sing decipherable lyrics. "At the time, the band was really into playing this song," says Montgomery. "Every chance they got, they played this song—at soundcheck, in the studio. I think that might have been Dave's influence. Dave was really into playing this; he was really into playing this type of drum beat. It is like a signature Dave Grohl drum beat." As the song was not yet officially recorded, the band allowed themselves a little leeway when performing it; when they played the song at their next live show in Rio, it developed into an extended jam that lasted nearly 20 minutes.

The song was also indicative of the harsher nature of many of the songs on *In Utero*. "There were some things that initially appeared as jams between songs and eventually evolved into songs," says Bailey. "But in terms of stuff that was cohesive and completely worked out, 'All Apologies' and 'Heart-Shaped Box' were some of the first things to emerge that you knew were going to be on the next release. The other stuff, things like 'Scentless Apprentice,' were so different from anything on *Bleach* or *Nevermind*, that you weren't really sure if this was somewhere they were going, or if this was something that was going to get shuffled aside later on."

The rest of the songs recorded at the sessions were along similar lines, abrasive and, indeed, punishing, in sharp contrast to the band's more pop-influenced, tuneful work. "Milk It" also uses the Nirvana formula of a softer verse/harder chorus, but here even the verses are fraught with tension. "At the time that they did this, it struck me that they were just kind of making it up," says Montgomery. "So I was surprised when I heard *In Utero* that this was relatively unchanged. They must have liked how it came out, because at the time it didn't feel like they really knew what they were doing; it had the feeling of something they were coming up with on the spot, like they were just working it out—just playing off each other and seeing where it went. It seemed pretty improv." Much the same could be said of "Moist Vagina," which lyrically consisted of little more than the title (though like "Milk It," the lyrics were not yet finalized), coupled with extremely heavy guitar work. "I think this was pretty off the cuff too," says Montgomery. "There's a bunch of stuff like this. I could definitely tell the difference between the songs that had been around, and this stuff. This was fun and catchy, though. But it's not much of a musical idea. It's a throwaway, I thought. It's a B-side. I just thought it was funny." Both versions of the two songs appeared on *With the Lights Out.*

I Hate Myself and I Want to Die had been one of Cobain's provisional titles for *In Utero*, though he insisted he meant it as "nothing more than a joke." The song that eventually took that title had no name when it was first recorded in Brazil, and begins with over a minute of noisy guitar feedback. But the song itself has a catchy melody, which suggests it could have been crafted into something stronger, had Cobain been interested in developing it further. "I love this one," Montgomery admits. "I like the riff and the rhythm. It actually has different music in the verse than in the chorus, which they weren't doing a lot anymore, but that's not why I liked it. I just liked it because I liked it. They looked like they were having fun when they were playing this song. I thought this could have been a hit. It kind of reminded me of a song from *Bleach*—like it could have been from that era." The song was released on *With the Lights Out*. The liner notes incorrectly say this version had previously appeared on *The Beavis and Butthead Experience*; it was actually released for the first time on *With the Lights Out*.

"Very Ape" opens with an irresistible hook straight out of the new wave era—hence the song's provisional title, "Perky New Wave." The song blends right into a lengthy improvisational number, possibly as the result of Montgomery's suddenly turning the tape machine on. "Part of the sessions were set aside for unstructured jamming," he explains. "So at those times I wasn't going to necessarily run 24-track tape, I would just run DAT. But if I thought they were doing something good, I would start the multi-track. So that may have been what happened here." The number was originally called "I'll Take You Down to the Pavement," a reference to an altercation between Cobain and Guns N' Roses lead singer Axl Rose at the MTV Video Music Awards the previous September 9, but was later retitled "Gallons of Rubbing Alcohol Flow Through the Strip." The track meanders along for over nine minutes, with Cobain alternating between seemingly disconnected singing and spoken-word sections, with Novoselic and Grohl providing a steady background accompaniment, punctuated by occasional bursts of noisy guitar. "That was just fucking around," says Novoselic.

"Gallons" and the remaining numbers recorded at the

session were not demos of future songs; they're simply examples of the kind of jams the band indulged in during rehearsals. Such moments were rarely captured in the studio, especially during the band's early years, when studio time was devoted to recording the required songs as quickly as possible. What both "Gallons" and the other main improvisational number recorded during the sessions do offer is a look at Cobain's, and the band's, more experimental side that was infrequently displayed on their records or in their live shows. "We should've recorded every rehearsal," says Novoselic. "'Cause sometimes we would rehearse and go through the songs and be really working, play all our songs twice, sometimes we'd work on new songs, and sometimes we'd just go in there and play free form. And there's only a few examples of that." The rambling, stream-of-consciousness lyrics also mirrored the writings in Cobain's journals.

"Gallons" was later released as a bonus "secret" track on non-US copies of *In Utero*, coming on twenty minutes after the final song on the album, in the same way "Endless Nameless" had appeared on *Nevermind*, coming on ten minutes after the purported last track, "Something in the Way," had finished. But while "Endless Nameless" had not been listed on the sleeve, and thus was truly a hidden track, the title of "Gallons" was on the sleeve, and additionally referred to as a "Devalued American Dollar Purchase Incentive Track" on the album's front cover as well. "They didn't want the United States version of the record competing with the European version," explains Novoselic. "So the European version needed added value on it."

The next number recorded was never given a final title, and was simply called "The Other Improv" when it was finally released on *With the Lights Out*. The number is essentially the same as "Gallons," though it's far less focused; the music plods along aimlessly, as does Cobain's accompanying vocal, which again alternates between singing and spoken word (the only part of which stands out is a cryptic reference to "my death certificate"). "This is just improv, trying to come up with something," says Montgomery. "I think he had a vague idea in his head; you could see that it could have been developed into something eventually. But this is just melodic ideas without even words or syllables. Krist can't even follow him because he doesn't know where he's going. Dave's just trying to feel along with him."

Two more numbers were also recorded at the sessions. One, variously known as "Meat" or "Dave's Meat Song," turned out to be a cover of "Onward into Countless Battles" by the Swedish heavy metal band Unleashed. Grohl recorded the song on his own while waiting for the rest of the band to show up, playing all the instruments himself. It's not dissimilar to the material he'd later record for his Probot side-project, consisting of power riffing and the thunderous repetition of the word "Meat!" Both Grohl and Cobain recorded themselves listing different types of meat in child-like voices, while Novoselic filmed them; a clip of this session appears on *With the Lights Out*'s DVD.

The DVD also features the group recording the last song of the sessions, a cover of Terry Jacks' "Seasons in the Sun." The morbid song about a young man dying had been a #1 in 1974, and was the first single Cobain had purchased. "It was just something that they wanted to do for fun," says Montgomery of the song. "They were into old, cheesy pop music and one-hit wonder stuff. We used to listen to ABBA all day in the van. Kurt definitely had that side to him. He was into pop music." The group also swapped instruments for the recording, with Cobain on drums (he also sang, though he forgot most of the song's words), Novoselic on guitar, and Grohl on bass.

The recording had been done quickly. "I think a lot of it happened the first day," says Montgomery. "Once we got rolling here, they just ran through all of it. I think it's all pretty much one take. Then maybe later or the second day was more of the improv stuff. I think by then some people didn't want to be there anymore and they just got out of there. So it was pretty quick, technically, once we got it working." The atmosphere was also markedly different to the October '92 sessions, and everyone was pleased with what had been achieved. "I remember being happy with it sonically, as far as the instruments that we got on tape," Montgomery says. "As far as the band, I think that they accomplished all that they set out to do. They didn't even use all of the time that they had. We had time left over [during which Love recorded songs for her band, Hole]. They just wanted to throw down their ideas to give them to Steve." By this time, the band had recorded demos in some form for all but one of the songs that would appear on *In Utero*. In just over three weeks, the final recording sessions would begin.

Chapter 6
The *In Utero* Sessions

Even before Nirvana had signed to DGC, Cobain had been toying with the idea of working with Steve Albini. "We were driving to Madison [Wisconsin] back in '90," Novoselic recalls (where the group would first work with Butch Vig). "And we were listening to something produced by Steve Albini, I think *Surfer Rosa* by the Pixies. By that time we were pulling all our gear in a trailer, so the van was nice and open, and there was this little couch against the back door. And Kurt lifted up his finger and he goes, 'And our snare sound will sound like this!' It was like he proclaimed it, 'cause he was sitting on that couch like he was a ruler on a throne. And then the tire blew out!"

Albini was himself a musician, having been a member of the abrasive Big Black and the provocatively named Rapeman. He was also a producer, though, like Jack Endino, he preferred to use the credit "Recorded By." Along with

Surfer Rosa, the Breeders' *Pod* was another Albini-produced album that was a favorite of Cobain's; he had also produced Jesus Lizard, Naked Raygun, and Jon Spencer Blues Explosion, among many others. In addition, he had a reputation as someone who did not suffer fools gladly, and was blunt about his dislike of the machinations of the mainstream music industry. "I'm not interested in being a part of the music business," he says. "I don't want to develop any relationships with any of these players, these administrative types, record label people. By and large those people are scum; I don't want to have anything to do with them."

Cobain had first seen Albini at Big Black's last show, which was held August 9, 1987 at the Georgetown Steamplant in Seattle. Though he would later tell a journalist he was not really "much of a Big Black fan," he had liked Albini's other work, and after the success of *Nevermind*, the band was interested in achieving a harsher sound in their recordings that better reflected their musical roots. "It was our sophomore [major label] record," says Novoselic. "And everybody was watching. So we thought, let's make a real indie record." The April '92 sessions at the Laundry Room and the January '93 sessions in Brazil had shown that they could still get back to cranking out songs quickly, as in their days at Sub Pop. The release of *Incesticide*, a collection of material from the band's early years, at the end of '92, served as a reminder to their new fans that Nirvana's music had not always had the slickness of the songs on *Nevermind*. The appeal of working with someone like the no-nonsense Albini, who had plenty of indie credibility, was obvious.

The band had spoken publicly about wanting to use Albini so frequently throughout '92 that rumors were circulating that he was officially signed on to produce the album. The problem was that Albini himself had not been contacted about the matter. "The press reported that repeatedly," he says. "I was having to contend with it on a daily basis. People were asking me about it, not just passers-by, but prospective clients, other bands, and it was genuinely affecting my business. So I sent the paper a letter saying, 'I have not been contacted by Nirvana, you didn't contact me before you printed this.'" Albini's denial was published—after which he finally was contacted by the band's management.

Albini had never seen the group live, though he was friends with Sub Pop's co-founder, Bruce Pavitt. "I remember him being all excited about Nirvana," he says. "I was aware of a lot of the things that had happened around that band, and I had heard their record and stuff, but I didn't count myself as a fan. The thing that changed my mind about their validity was seeing them work in the studio."

Albini had preliminary talks with both Cobain and Grohl, "just discussing the approach to making the record and talking to them about records they liked and stuff that I should listen to to acquaint myself with what they wanted to try to do," he says. "It seemed like they wanted to make precisely the sort of record that I'm comfortable doing, and it seemed like they genuinely liked the records that I did make, so the whole thing seemed legitimate to me. The reason I decided to do it was I not only got the impression they were genuine about wanting me to work on it, they were also genuine about wanting to make a record for themselves. That's really all I cared about. I didn't want to be in a position where we were trying to satisfy some outside agency. And I didn't know if they would be allowed to make a record that way. I just figured, if they make a record and give it to their record label, then they will be in a much better situation on an emotional level, and the record will go faster and be better than if they try to make a record where they're trying to clear obstacles with the record label the entire way and trying to get people to rubber stamp it. So I asked the band if I could deal with them directly, and not have to contend with the record label at all, and they said, 'Yes, that's fine.' So all of my dealings were with the band. To this day, I don't honestly know if anyone from Geffen has ever spoken to me."

But he admits that agreeing to work on the album after denying he was doing so, "sort of created the first of many little micro-controversies. Once it was apparent that I was working on the record, it seemed like I had tried to create some sort of Nixonian denial of it, so that if everything went shitty, I could get out of it without ever having been publicly associated with it. That was the beginning of a pretty bizarre period, where my parents, among other people, who had been mercifully insulated from most of everything to do with the music scene, started reading things in the daily newspaper in Montana [where Albini was raised] about me working on this record or some other overboiled micro-controversy. That was the beginning of the 'weird' period."

And Albini's suspicions about the "outside agencies" Nirvana worked with were not inaccurate; those close to the band were none too pleased with their choice of producer. "I don't think they were too happy about it, because Albini's such an iconoclast," Novoselic confirms. "He's an outspoken critic of the major labels, and excess, of musical pomp and excess." Nor were the band's artistic desires taken very seriously by those around them. In trying to reassure Gary Gersh, the band's A&R rep, about Albini, Grohl recalled to writer Phil Sutcliffe, "I said, 'Gary, man, don't be so afraid, the record will turn out great!' He said, 'Oh, I'm not afraid, go ahead, bring me back the best you can do.' It was like, 'Go and have your fun, then we'll get another producer and make the *real* album'" (emphasis Grohl's).

But if the label felt the band was wasting their time, they had to concede they weren't wasting money; Albini's fee was a modest $100,000, and he refused to take any royalties ("Anyone who takes a royalty off a band's record—other than someone who actually writes music or plays on the record—is a thief," he told Azerrad). They would also be recording at the same place Albini had recently finished working with PJ Harvey on *Rid of Me*, Pachyderm Studios, located just outside the small town of Cannon Falls, 40 miles southeast of Minneapolis, Minnesota. It was felt that the remote location would cut down on outside distractions, and it was also inexpensive—recording costs were said to be a mere $24,000. Albini sent Cobain a copy of *Rid of Me* to give him an idea of what the studio sounded like.

Albini had also been sent a cassette by the group, of the songs they had worked on in Brazil. "I preferred them immediately to the stuff that I had heard of *Nevermind*," he says. "The *Nevermind* album seemed very confined in its parameters. Each song had a beginning, middle, and an end, and it was all presented in a way that allowed you to hear each chunk. This new material, some of it was kind of sprawling and aimless, and I liked that, but there were still moments that were really powerful and dynamic. It just seemed like they had made a conceptual break in how they wanted to be and how they wanted to behave as a band, and what they wanted their music to sound like."

Just before leaving, there was a last minute equipment crisis. "The night before they flew out I got this panicked phone call," says Earnie Bailey. "They were practicing the night before and Kurt said that his Echo Flanger was broken. When those things break, they're really complex under the hood, and I don't want to say poorly made, but they weren't built to the highest standards. Kurt said, 'It's the entire album—it's *got* to work!' He had been using his Echo

Flanger to do all of this material, and I think he was worried that it wouldn't sound the same. So I said that I would take a look it. We met over at Krist's house, and it was really funny, because they popped the pedal open, and all he'd really done was he'd bumped the AC switch that turns the power on with his foot! It was hilarious, because it was such a simple fix. I was able to fix it with a Phillips screwdriver and a pair of pliers, and the level of gratitude was ridiculous. 'Man, you saved the album!' I had to laugh because I was like, 'Man, this is the easiest thing I've ever done.'"

The band, booked into Pachyderm as "The Simon Ritchie Bluegrass Ensemble," arrived in Minnesota the second week in February. The studio grounds also had a large house where clients could stay, another factor that helped the group focus on their work. "We were isolated," says Novoselic. "I don't know how we survived through that. It was pretty mellow. For two weeks, we were in this house, cooped up in the middle of nowhere, like a gulag. There was snow outside, we couldn't go anywhere. We just worked."

Recording began on February 13, and most days the group adhered to a regular schedule, beginning work around midday, taking a dinner break, then continuing to work until around midnight. "It was pretty simple, straight ahead," says Novoselic. "It was pretty live. Some of those songs were first takes." Their work ethic impressed Albini. "We earned his respect," says Novoselic. "'Cause he would stand there by the tape machine with his arms folded. And we'd play most of the songs in the first, second take, and he'd nod his head, like all right, these guys are the real thing."

There was a moment when Bailey's services were thought to be required. "I got a call the day or two after they arrived and they were having some kind of trouble getting going," he says. "I wasn't really sure what it was about, if it was problems tuning—I don't know if they didn't want to be bothered tuning their own stuff and didn't really feel like it would be a big deal having me along. So they arranged for me to fly out and I was waiting for the call, and then I spoke with Krist on the phone and he said that most of the instrument tracking was finished! They pounded out most of the album very quickly; I wasn't expecting Fleetwood Mac's *Rumours*, but I wasn't expecting it to happen that fast either. I remember being really excited by that, just thinking that they were doing something that raw and spontaneous and not being so critical that they were going to go over everything and kill it, you know?"

As usual, most of the album's lyrics were worked on up to the point of recording; Albini remembers Cobain carrying around a notebook of potential lyrics. "Many people would be expecting me to be writing about the last two years and my past experiences—drugs, having a child, the press coming down on us and stuff like that," he told a journalist a month before the album's release. "There's a little bit of my life on [the album], but for the most part it's very impersonal." It was a remarkably disingenuous claim, for Cobain's recent experiences permeated virtually every track on the record. The key events in his life the previous year had been the success of his band and the resultant media frenzy that had caused, his struggles with drugs, and the birth of his daughter. Accordingly, the record was replete with references to babies, childbirth, and reproduction (the album's very title means "in the womb"), witch hunts, the loss of privacy, illness and disease, and ambivalence about fame. The songs expressed a heartfelt anguish that would later cause some to interpret the entire album as a cry for help, but even at the time of its release *In Utero* could easily be read as an album focused on physical and spiritual sickness. But *In Utero*'s saving grace is that it doesn't fully give in to despair; the bursts of anger and sarcasm throughout the album keep the songs from sinking into abject despondency. Rather than being overwhelmed by circumstances, Cobain's songs on *In Utero* show him—for the most part—still able and willing to fight back. As such, among Nirvana's recorded efforts, it stands as Cobain's most personal work.

The first song on the first tape box from the sessions, dated February 13, is "Chuck Chuck Fo Fuck," an obvious reference to the rhythm of the song's main riff, and only meant as a temporary title; by the end of the sessions it was retitled "Scentless Apprentice." The song was inspired by Patrick Süskind's best-selling novel *Perfume: The Story of a Murderer*. Set in 18th century France, the novel is the story of a man whose own body has no scent, but who has a highly developed sense of smell; apprenticed to a perfumer, his quest to capture the "ultimate perfume" of virgin women leads him to commit murder.

Appropriately, the song is one of *In Utero*'s most aggressive, alternating between the "chuck chuck" riff Grohl had come up with and Cobain's ascending answer call, underpinned by Novoselic's steady bass line and Grohl's powerful drumming. "It's a good example of the Nirvana dynamic at work," says Novoselic. "There's three players but there's a lot of stuff going on." The verses have allusions to the book's storyline, but it's the chorus that captures the attention here. Cobain seems to sum up not only the misanthropy of the book's lead character, but also his own, in his tortured shrieks of "Go away!" ("I just wanted to be as far away from people as I could—their smells disgust me," he told Azerrad in discussing the song.) As he reaches the end of each scream, his anger boils over into pure rage and his voice virtually gives out, in one of Cobain's most tortured and anguished performances. The song is one of the few in Nirvana's catalogue where the music is credited to all three members.

Bodily excretions and illness are the focus of "Milk It," initially entitled "PiL" (presumably after John Lydon's first post-Sex Pistols band), and then "Milk Made." It's a stark portrait of dependency with near-mumbled verses, dotted with words like "parasite," "endorphins," and "virus," none of which were in the version recorded in Brazil; at other points the lyrics are seemingly nothing more than random wordplay. The verses explode into maelstroms of noise and screams as they surge into the choruses, though the fury is somewhat tempered by Cobain's brief chuckle before the final chorus. But the overall bleakness of the scenario is confirmed by the observation that the only "bright side" in the future is suicide, the song screeching to a halt after Cobain's final screams.

"That's a gnarly song," says Novoselic. "The lyrics are pretty heavy. I got the bass nailed and real steady in a way that kind of harks back to 'Teen Spirit.' It's the same formula, but it's way twisted, kind of grotesque—it's a grotesque song."

Yet the twisted elements in both this song and "Scentless Apprentice" are what most impressed their producer. "There's always one or two songs on any given session that strike you as being the money shot, like, 'Wow, this is an amazing song, this is where everything came together, and this is really great,'" says Albini. "For me, that was the 'Milk Made' song or whatever it ended up being called, and 'Scentless Apprentice.' Those are the two that struck me as being the biggest step for the band. They seemed like the biggest break with their aggressive pop style that they were developing for themselves. They seemed the most adventurous sonically, and the most up my alley anyway." Being newer songs, both were also perhaps more indicative of the future direction Nirvana would have pursued. In 2005,

Grohl cited both "Milk It" and "Heart-Shaped Box" as his favorite Nirvana songs.

In recording the songs, Albini also recalls, "On both of those, there were two vocal takes. There was one take that was singing the whole of the song, and one take where Kurt was just singing parts of the song to emphasize them or parts of the song with a different sound quality. There's a really dry, really loud voice that comes zooming up at the end of 'Milk It,' a vocal that's really dry and uncomfortably loud. That was something that was also done at the end of 'Rape Me,' where he wanted the sound of him screaming to just overtake the whole of the band." Though Cobain's screams were long noted for being key to Nirvana's sound, nothing the band previously recorded matched the sheer intensity of the vocal performances on *In Utero*.

There was then another go at "Sappy." It was a very unusual choice for the sessions, as the group hadn't played the song live since November 1990 (and after these sessions they would only play it a further three times). This version was the most fully produced band version of the song, slightly shorter than previous band versions, with a faster tempo and a noticeably stronger drum part. This version also begins without the instrumental intro on some of the earlier versions.

As for why the song was again revisited, Novoselic says simply, "We liked to play that song. I put that bass line together four years before that, and I thought it was really great, so I never changed it. It seems like nobody ever changed anything else on it either. You can hear older versions of, like, 'Lithium' or whatever, the bass lines are different, or the guitars, something's different. But why is it that this song, every time we recorded it, everybody did everything exactly the same? Well, I was totally happy with it, so why change it?"

Actually, the song was not "exactly the same" each time the group recorded it. There were always some variations—the Albini version featured a different guitar solo in the instrumental break, and was in a different key—though they were admittedly minor ones. And there still remained some dissatisfaction with it, as "Sappy" didn't appear on any of the proposed track listings for the album. "I actually think it's a pretty good song," is Albini's summation. "I don't remember it being bad. But I think it wore out its welcome on the band, apparently."

Next was "Very Ape," then still titled "Perky New Wave," which would be one of the shortest on *In Utero*. It's essentially the same length as the acoustic home demo of the song featured on *With the Lights Out*, said to have been recorded in 1993, with lyrics that appear to be similar to the version recorded in Brazil. But while the musical structure on the home demo, Brazil version, and the Albini version is basically the same (though the Albini version has a tighter performance), the lyric on the Albini version is vastly different. In the end, "Very Ape" is a send-up of stereotypical macho behavior, *à la* "Mr. Moustache" on *Bleach*; it's the singer himself who's regressively "very ape," primitive, hiding his naivety behind a wall of braggadocio. Musically, the song's most interesting aspect is the persistent new wave-flavored riff that wails through the song like a siren, not dissimilar from the main riff in "Lounge Act" from *Nevermind*. The jerky rhythms also bring new wave act Devo to mind, one of the few groups whose songs Nirvana covered.

February 14 saw the first run-through of "Pennyroyal Tea," the first take an instrumental. The song had been written during the winter of 1990-91, when Cobain was then sharing an apartment with Grohl in Olympia, Washington. But though it was first performed on April 17, 1991 at the same show where "Smells Like Teen Spirit" had its public debut, and the group subsequently performed it on their fall '91 tour, the song was apparently not considered for *Nevermind*. Cobain later told Azerrad the song was written "in about thirty seconds," the lyrics taking somewhat longer —half an hour. "I remember hearing it and thinking, 'God, this guy has such a beautiful sense of melody, I can't believe he's screaming all the time,'" Grohl later told *Harp* magazine.

As there was little lyrical variation in the song from '91 to '93 (the lyrics on the home demo on *With the Lights Out*, said to be from 1993, are identical to the released version), the instrumental version recorded with Endino was presumably just intended to nail down the musical arrangement. The verses convey a profound sense of anomie, with each one mentioning some ailment or at the very least disaffectedness (as in the second verse's wonderful longing for a "Leonard Cohen afterworld"). The final verse, with its references to warm milk, laxatives, and antacids, touches on Cobain's well-documented stomach problems, which caused him pain throughout much of his life, but were never properly diagnosed. ("I'm always in pain, and that adds to the anger in our music," he told writer Jon Savage. "I'm grateful to it, in a way.")

The song's title refers to a home abortion method, though the lyric extended what Cobain called its "cleansing theme" to a hope it would wash away one's inner demons, in addition to being a means of eliminating something that was "in utero." And while the song has the Nirvana formula of quiet verses/loud choruses, Cobain's vocal during the chorus still has a lugubrious feel (with the harmonizing vocals adding a degree of tension), as if the singer is suspended in some stage between sleep and wakefulness (also tying in with the song's references to insomnia). This element was something that would be even more apparent in the *Unplugged* performance of the song. His summation of being "anemic royalty" was an image that was indicative of his own contradictory nature; being powerful, yet feeling powerless.

"Radio Friendly Unit Shifter" was titled both "You Said a Mouthful" and "Nine Month Media Blackout" on the tape box, and elsewhere was also referred to "Four Month Media

Blackout" (though while interviews with the band were limited from 1992 on, there was never any official media blackout). A "Radio Friendly Unit Shifter" refers to songs that are both accessible and strong sellers—a hit single, in other words. In any case, the lyrics don't really reflect any of the titles, and are more reflective of what Cobain insisted was his usual songwriting method—stringing together lines he found in his journals. But there are a few lines that hint at a more personal meaning. There's a pointed reference to privacy, as well as the childbirth imagery ("my water broke"). And the desperation of the chorus, which repeatedly begs to know what's wrong, is matched by a bridge that expresses a measure of hopefulness—find where you belong, and the truth shall set you free.

The song begins with a wailing guitar note, then, as Novoselic admits, "There's just one riff through the whole song! I pretty much just play the same riff through the whole song." Nonetheless, the song's propulsive energy is undeniable, and though Novoselic calls the title "cynical, sarcastic," there's also some truth in it—the song has a catchiness that is accessible (something the group recognized by opening virtually every subsequent show with the song). Tellingly, the song didn't get its final title until after the band's label had told the group that the album wasn't "radio friendly" enough.

"Frances Farmer Will Have Her Revenge on Seattle" was a song that "came to the band pretty intact," says

Novoselic. "Kurt brought it in pretty finished. Lyrics were left to last. That's why in practice tapes you hear Kurt singing phonetically, just doing the melody." Like "Scentless Apprentice," "Frances Farmer" was inspired by a book, *Shadowland*, William Arnold's autobiography of the actress, published in 1978. Farmer was born in Seattle in 1914. In the 1930s she found fame in such films as *Come and Get It*, but following an arrest for drunken driving in 1942, her life was set on a downward spiral that resulted in her being committed to a mental institution and lobotomized. She died of cancer of the esophagus in 1970.

Cobain had been fascinated by Farmer's story since reading Arnold's book in high school. And after he himself became a star, he identified even more with her story, especially with Farmer's unconventional nature, her outspoken dislike of commercialism, her hounding by the media, and her sad, unjust fate. Arnold worked as a film critic at the *Seattle Post-Intelligencer*, a daily newspaper, and Cobain made several attempts to contact him in 1993. When he didn't respond, Cobain contacted the Arts and Entertainment editor at the paper, who passed the message on to Arnold. "I said, 'Who is Kurt Cobain?'" he recalls. "She was shocked that I didn't know who he was."

Arnold had not responded as he'd been pestered by "hundreds" of obsessed people about Farmer since the book's publication, and he figured that Cobain was just another of them. But Cobain was persistent. "He called and left this rambling message," Arnold says. "I have this vague memory of him saying he had read this book when he was in high school and he got it from the Aberdeen library. It had a big impact on him. And there was something about him thinking he was related to Judge Frater [who signed the first court order to commit Farmer], and just rambling. I thought to myself, 'I've really got to talk to this guy,' but I was going through other stuff then and I just didn't. Then he killed himself and I felt really bad."

Arnold didn't hear the song until after Cobain's death, and he also wrote a short piece about his missed communications with Cobain. "The weird thing to me is the lesson that when you write stuff, you do influence people in ways that you don't even know," he says. "And that gives you a certain moral responsibility. I don't know what that responsibility is, and I don't know how far you can carry it, but you have that responsibility, whether you like it or not. You can't just say, 'Well, I don't care,' because people can take it any way they want to." It was an observation Cobain might well have benefited from, given his frequent comments he wished there was a "Rock Star 101" course he could've taken to adjust to his unexpected fame.

Instead, "Frances Farmer" seethes with controlled anger, as Cobain drew parallels between the unfair treatment he felt he and his wife had experienced under the scrutiny of "false witnesses" and what Farmer had endured (unsurprisingly, he also draws on witch hunt imagery). But it's also a song of vengeance, with Farmer returning to scorch her enemies into oblivion, a rare case of someone emerging triumphant in a Nirvana song. But such solace eludes the singer himself, who prefers to sink into oblivion, longing for the "comfort in being sad."

The version of "Moist Vagina" recorded at the Albini sessions was not markedly different from the one recorded in Brazil, though the Albini version has a final minute of noise concluding with what sounds like a dry gargle from Cobain. In essence, it's a slightly more melodic version of the improv material Nirvana recorded in Brazil, and though the title and its harsh music wouldn't have made it out of place on *In Utero*, it was apparently never considered for the album's final lineup. Nor was it ever known to have been played live. Perhaps, as in the jams played during the last session with Endino, it was only meant as a means of taking a break.

"Punk Rock," later called "tourette's," is a song that Novoselic says dates back to the Go Team era, the Go Team being an ad hoc collection of Olympia musicians that Cobain recorded a single with. It has the distinction of being *In Utero*'s shortest track, one minute and thirty-three seconds of pure sonic assault, after the jokey spoken intro, "Moderate rock!" The final name, "tourette's," refers to Gilles de la Tourette syndrome, more commonly called Tourette's syndrome, a condition that compels the sufferer to involuntarily blurt out obscenities. Cobain may well be

screaming obscenities during the song, but it's hard to tell—
the most distinguishable word is "Hey!" The music itself
consists of a four note riff pounded out repetitively; this
version is a good 40 seconds shorter than the instrumental
take recorded with Endino, simply cutting back on some of
the repetitions. Cobain himself admitted to writer Dave
Thompson the number "isn't that good a song" but it
nonetheless made the final cut because "it fit the mood."

The band then made a first attempt at what was arguably
the defining track of the album, "Heart-Shaped Box."
Cobain wrote the song in early '92, but then had trouble
developing it with the band. Before putting it aside for good,
he decided to have the band jam on it once again and this
time it came together, "instantly," Cobain said. This clearly
occurred before the Brazil session, by which time the bulk
of the song had been worked out.

"Heart-Shaped Box" was the Nirvana formula personi-
fied, with a restrained, descending riff played through the
verse, building in intensity to the cascading passion of the
chorus. Cobain told Azerrad the song's "basic idea" was
about children with cancer, a topic which made him unbear-
ably sad. But while the song does reference the illness, the
lyrics appear more to address the physical and emotional
dependencies inherent in relationships. The imagery is particularly striking, with phrases like "tar pit trap," "meat-eat-
ing orchids," and "umbilical noose." That these female symbols each hold a potential danger means they all convey a

fear that ultimately equates intimacy with a suffocating claustrophobia. Yet the singer is unable, or unwilling, to tear himself away, snarling at his own submissiveness in the sarcastic chorus. Cobain's vocal on the song is one of his most evocative. The fact that so many of Nirvana's songs end in strenuous screaming means that his emotive delivery in quieter moments is sometimes overlooked, as in the haunting way his voice slightly catches while singing the words "baby's breath" or "highness," contrasting with the manic glee with which he sings of his newest complaints in the chorus. Another of the song's inspirations was the heart-shaped box filled with seashells, teacups, pinecones, and a doll that had been Love's first gift to her future husband.

Though pleased with the performance on the whole, Novoselic strenuously objected to a shimmering effect used on the guitar solo that he found "really grating. These were the words I said: 'Why do you want to take such a beautiful song and throw this hideous abortion in the middle of it?' And they're like, 'Well, I don't know, it sounds good.' They didn't have any good arguments, because they were sabotaging it is what they were doing. Kurt was being self-conscious. 'Why can't you just make it beautiful?' 'I don't know.' I argued and argued and argued and argued about it, and they just wouldn't listen." Novoselic's assessment was right; the discordant sound of the effect broke the haunting mood of the song.

Also recorded on the 14th was another song destined

to be as anthemic as "Heart-Shaped Box"—a song then called "La La La," but ultimately titled "All Apologies." This version was more stripped down than the version recorded in 1991 with Craig Montgomery, without extra touches like the tambourine. Like "Radio Friendly Unit Shifter," the number is deceptively simple, with a single insinuating melodic line played throughout most of it. But again, the strength of the performance keeps the song from sounding repetitive, due in part to the addition of a bittersweet cello line (played by Kera Schaley, the only other musician to appear on the record).

Cobain's lyric and resigned delivery also invest the song with an elegiac quality. In the verses, the singer effectively takes all the problems of the world on his shoulders, assuming all the blame, even turning his back on his work, in a song that's wracked with guilt (though Cobain insisted it was "a very, very sarcastic song"). As in "Dumb," the narrator is caught looking in from the outside, torn between the desire to be included and the urge to maintain the independence of standing alone. It was a conflict Cobain never worked out, and after his death, more than one observer described this song as being akin to a suicide note. Again, there's a glimmer of hope in the chorus, with the singer finding some sense of unity with the sun, though singing of being married as being "buried" was a comparison that would inevitably result in media speculation about the state of Cobain's own marriage —exactly the kind of attention he disparaged on the rest of the album (in interviews, he said he wrote the lines before meeting Love).

"I remember really liking the sound of that song as a contrast to the more aggressive ones," says Albini. "I remember thinking it sounded really good in that it sounded lighter, but it didn't sound conventional. It was sort of a crude light sound that suited the band."

On the 15th, the group recorded the song that would eventually be titled "I Hate Myself and I Want to Die" but on the tape box was represented by a drawing of a fish. "That was just one of those dirty little songs that we'd do," says Novoselic. "They're just really fucked up, demented. They're trashy, but they're tight; they have a lot of good energy. They're catchy." The song is largely the same as the version recorded in Brazil, minus the lengthy intro, and with a different guitar solo. Musically, it occupies a middle ground between *In Utero*'s more aggressive material and songs like "Heart-Shaped Box" and "Pennyroyal Tea"; the underlying pop sensibility makes it not unpleasant to listen to, though lyrically it remains unmemorable. Nor was it apparently of much interest to the band; Cobain dismissed it as "a typical, boring song," and they never performed it live. The group also put together a version with a jokey spoken-word vocal overdubbed on the main track.

Then came "Rape Me," which was written around the time of the *Nevermind* sessions and was performed during the fall 1991 tour. By the time the song was released, it was easy to read it as a condemnation of the media harassment Cobain felt he had suffered, especially as the song's intro reworks the opening chords of the group's biggest hit, "Smells Like Teen Spirit." But in fact most of the lyric was complete before *Nevermind* was even released, though Cobain conceded the "favorite inside source" line, added to the bridge later, was intended as a direct jab at the media (among the album's thank-yous was a listing for "Our favorite inside sources across the globe").

Interestingly, the acoustic demo of the song on *With the Lights Out*, said to have been recorded in 1992, has different lyrics; curious, as the song had already been performed in concert with the same lyrics that would be used in the *In Utero* version. The verses seemingly welcome abuse, though there is an implied threat of comeuppance in Cobain's grim delivery. This was something that was particularly true of the song's ending; as in "Milk It," Cobain's vocal was recorded so that it "just overwhelms the band and becomes this really uncomfortable presence," says Albini, though "frightening" would be a more appropriate description than "uncomfortable."

The end result was a song that was part submissive invitation, part defiant taunt, a mix that confused and disturbed many listeners. Cobain found himself having to explain repeatedly that the song was not meant to advocate assault of any kind; "It's an anti-, let me repeat that, anti-rape song," he patiently explained to MTV. That there were still those who missed the point was evidenced by the fact that *In Utero* was initially banned in Singapore and South Korea because of the track and other profanities on the album. In a letter to the South Korean authorities, the band's manager, John Silva, stressed the song's relation to media harassment, writing, "[Cobain] used the analogy of a 'rape' to highlight the degree to which he felt violated as a result of his newfound celebrity." His justification for the use of the word "shit" in "Milk It" was more convoluted, stating the song addressed the exploitation of Cobain's talent by a greedy music industry; "When taken on face value with a predisposition towards subjective language requirements, I think you'll agree that the effectiveness of this song is due largely to the graphic nature of this [obscene] refrain," Silva wrote.

"Serve the Servants" is a song that Novoselic remembers Cobain bringing in "pretty much done" (it's the only song on *In Utero* that wasn't previously demoed by the band). It was also a song that was his most openly autobiographical, as even Cobain had to admit—the first two verses dealing with the aftermath of fame, the second two with family. Musically, the track was a straight-ahead rock song, arguably the most straightforward on *In Utero*, with the tempo steady throughout, as is the volume, in a departure from the soft/loud Nirvana formula.

Cobain's sense of persecution is made clear when he again likens his targeting by the "self-appointed judges" of the media to a witch-hunt in the first verse. His portrayal of his troubled relationship with his father in the second verse revisits a familiar theme in his work, unhappiness with one's family, as in "Paper Cuts" from *Bleach* and "Even in His Youth," a 1991 B-side (in comparison, the home demo on *With the Lights Out* has completely different lyrics). Yet in the chorus, he sardonically dismisses the impact his parents' "legendary divorce" had on him, in the same way he claimed in interviews his own songs "don't have much personal meaning at all." But in this instance, Cobain's meaning was clear; "This is the way Nirvana's Kurt Cobain spells success: s-u-c-k-s-e-g-g-s," David Fricke wrote in his review of the album for *Rolling Stone*. But the question of why a young man who'd enjoyed such unexpected acclaim and monetary rewards now found himself left "bored and old" remained unanswered.

Two and a half years after it was written, "Dumb" was finally recorded. "That's a beautiful song," says Novoselic. "That's a really good one. I like the BBC version of that song [recorded in 1991, which features identical lyrics to the *In Utero* version]. It's real raw, but still the beauty is strong. A sweet pop song."

"Sweet" in sound perhaps, but dark in sentiment; "Dumb" has a lyric thoroughly steeped in melancholy. This time, the outsider is also a recluse, fully immersed—drowning?—in the "comfort in being sad," the same state that the narrator of "Frances Farmer" yearned to attain. Yet, as is true of many of the album's quieter songs, the sadness is laced with resignation, not despondency. The narrator is again on the outside looking in, and this time seems to be too filled with apathy to have much desire to change the situation. Cobain's world-weary vocal conveys the exhaustion of a man who hasn't slept for days, but is past caring—even when he sings of being happy (a highly unusual sentiment to be expressed in a Nirvana song), he qualifies that with a "maybe." The song is shorter than the instrumental recorded at Word of Mouth, eliminating one of the verse repetitions. A cello line adds a mellow undercurrent to the song's chorus and bridge.

Albini remembers Pachyderm's studio tech, Bob Weston, primarily working with Grohl on his material, which was recorded next. "Dave Solo" was a quick minute and a half of heavy metal-style riffing, along the same lines as "Dave's Meat Song," perhaps intended as a warm-up. It couldn't have made more of a contrast with what was called "Dave's Mellow Song," a song Grohl had already released as "Color Pictures of a Marigold."

Grohl had previously released the song in 1992 on his solo cassette *Pocketwatch*, recorded under the name Late!, on which he plays all instruments himself. This version of the song is shorter, and features better production, which heightens its delicate, brooding quality. Two instrumental versions were recorded before Grohl recorded one with vocals; when the song was released, it would surprise many who hadn't realized Grohl had been recording his own songs for years.

Following "Marigold" is another improv number, the instrumental "Lullaby." Organ, bass, and drums swirl around each other for three minutes in an aimless jam that ends with a spate of wild drumming.

On the 16th, more takes of "Pennyroyal Tea" and "Heart-Shaped Box" were recorded, and then the basic tracks for the album were completed. "Recording was very straightforward," says Albini. "They recorded the basic take as a band, all recorded live. And on almost every song, Kurt would add one, sometimes two additional little guitar parts. I would say that was basically it."

Cobain then recorded the vocals with dispatch (one account claims all vocals were laid down in six hours). By this time, he had become a far more expressive singer than he had been on *Bleach*, and without the double-tracking and other effects used on *Nevermind* one gets a far greater sense of what he was capable of as a vocalist. Especially notable is the immensity of his emotional range, from frenzied shrieks to a gentle, even soothing, delivery. Similarly, the album also highlights all three member's skill as musicians. Nirvana wasn't a one-note band that was only capable of rocking out; they were also a group that could actually play. The melodic strengths of Nirvana's songs were later clearly revealed in their *Unplugged* performance.

Mixing was done over the course of five days. "That was also very straightforward," Albini recalls. "We basically just pushed the faders up and take it at a decent balance, and then put it down. So we didn't really screw around a lot on any of it. I think we got two or three songs mixed every day."

The group took time to relax as well, going into Minneapolis to see the Cows one evening. They also made various prank phone calls. At one point Grohl called Silva, claiming that after three days he still doing a soundcheck on the snare drum—then having to rush to assure Silva he was only joking. Bailey was also kept up-to-date about the sessions. "Dave described to me at one point an idea that Albini had about hanging suspending microphones overhead and having them swing back and forth over his cymbals," he says. "I don't think that they ever utilized that, but it was an idea I was excited about because I liked the idea of something kind of chaotic in the recording like that." Courtney Love turned up during the second week of the sessions with Frances and there was some resulting friction. But overall, the working atmosphere was positive, with a camaraderie that was evident to Albini. "Kurt was the principle songwriter and he was the lead vocalist, but the other two guys in that band had far more to do with the ultimate sound and direction of the band than anyone has given them credit for," he says.

Albini also had a favorable impression of the members as people. "Dave and Kurt and Krist had a very overtly goofy take on things," he says. "I really liked and enjoyed their company. Kurt was more withdrawn initially, but I think that's only to be expected because he didn't know me; he didn't have any reason to trust me or whatever. I didn't try to get on any sort of intimate level with him, out of respect for the pressure he must feel under every day—having people try to get close to him all the time. I figured I'd allow him as much distance as he wanted. It was obvious that what was going on in his head was as important to him as what was going on between him and other people."

Novoselic suggested opening the album with one of the harsher tracks. "I wanted to start the record off with 'Scentless Apprentice,'" he recalls. "I remember saying, 'Let's get some mall rat girls that'll buy this record and just freak them out! And freak their moms out!' We were laughing." "Rape Me" was also considered as the opening track, but it was felt it would draw too much of a parallel to *Nevermind*, as that album's first track was the song the opening of "Rape Me" plays off of, "Teen Spirit." "I Hate Myself" was originally considered for the final lineup, but was dropped to keep the album from sounding too noisy; it later appeared on the compilation *The Beavis and Butthead Experience*. The remaining songs were apparently not considered for the album, but were released elsewhere: "Sappy," renamed "Verse Chorus Verse" appeared on the compilation *No Alternative*, and "Moist Vagina" and "Marigold" were used as B-sides.

Novoselic later told a journalist it took two weeks to decide the running order for the album. Ultimately, *In*

Utero's final running order would be: "Serve the Servants," "Scentless Apprentice," "Heart-Shaped Box," "Rape Me," "Frances Farmer Will Have Her Revenge on Seattle," "Dumb," "Very Ape," "Milk It," "Pennyroyal Tea," "Radio Friendly Unit Shifter," "tourette's," and "All Apologies."

The sessions were wrapped up by February 26, and everyone smoked cigars to celebrate. "It worked in precisely the same way as any session that I do," Albini says. "The band shows up, they know their material, they have their equipment together, they set up, they play, we add a few things, and we mix it. It was very, very straightforward." But the road to *In Utero*'s release would not be.

Chapter 7
The Album Mix

"I expected it to be like most of the other records I had done, where we finish the record, the record is released, and everybody is happy," is how Albini recalls he felt following the conclusion of the *In Utero* sessions. But in this instance, what should have been a straightforward matter soon degenerated into a blame game that eventually blew up to become a matter of national interest.

For a few weeks after Nirvana had completed the album, Albini heard nothing. Then, one day, "I got a phone call from a journalist in Chicago named Greg Kot [with the *Chicago Tribune*] who said that he'd just been speaking with Gary Gersh, and that Gary had told him that this Nirvana record I had made was unreleaseable and that it all was going to have to be redone, and what was my comment," he says. "I don't remember specifically what I told him, but I know I would have told him that Gary Gersh could go fuck himself.

"Well, within the circles of the people who had sort of a window peepers' interest in what happened with that record, news of that tiff went out like wildfire," Albini continues. "It seemed like everyone that I crossed paths with was aware of that argument and had an opinion on it. Most of them had advice for me, and most of them had advice for Nirvana, and none of it was really intelligent because it was all from a position of ignorance. From a certain perspective, I feel like *I* was speaking from a position of ignorance, because I wasn't there when the band was having their discussions with the record label. All I know is what my interaction with them was, which was, we made a record, everybody was happy with it. A few weeks later I hear that it's unreleasable and it's all got to be redone."

Kot never confirmed that Gersh was the source for his article, but Cobain later told several journalists that Gersh—among others—hadn't liked the record "for various sonic reasons," he explained to one writer. To *Melody Maker*, he said, "[Gersh] didn't think the songwriting was up to par. And having your A&R say that is kind of like having your father or stepfather telling you to take out the trash." Gersh himself, in a radio program, later said that on first listen he felt the album "could sound a lot better than it did," but stressed that "I heard it unfinished."

Still, the band members themselves were also starting to question the results the more they listened to the record, wondering if they had spent too little time in mixing. They also played it for close friends to solicit their opinions. "I remember Krist coming home with the first mix on a cassette," says Earnie Bailey, "and it was so strange, because here I am hearing this new album that was so anticipated, and it was like our lives were kind of hanging in the balance with this new album, and we're hearing it on a boom box in his kitchen. So it really didn't have much impact—you could barely hear what it was all about. I remember it was really exciting, but it sounded so much like a practice because Kurt was using virtually no effects; there's very little double tracking on his vocals. Everything is really, really dry. But I liked it. I remember just being in awe at the kind of risk they were going to take with this, putting out something that was really them. I mean, this was what they sounded like more or less live, and definitely what they sounded like at practice. So we were really excited about it."

When Charles Peterson was photographing the back cover collage of the album at Cobain's house, he also heard a version of the album. "Kurt played, I don't know if it was a rough mix, but he played a mix of *In Utero* for me," he says. "I thought it was great. He was really concerned about the mix; he's like, 'What do you think of the mix?' and I was like, 'I dunno, it sounds good to me.' But of course he was just playing it over a boom box in his kitchen, and I was trying to take photos of this collage before the flowers wilted. I remember distinctly 'Rape Me' as the song that really stood out, particularly lyrically wise. I just stopped photographing for a few minutes, and was like 'Whoa!'"

But Bailey also recalls the perception of the record changing over time. "I remember the first wave of feedback —everybody was really excited about it," he says. "Two or three days go by, and then the concerns started to come in— 'Well, we're not sure about this,' and 'We think that this should be changed.' Then it started to snowball a little bit. There was some nastiness about that; the band was like, 'We're not going to change the record, fuck you,' blah, blah, blah. Then a couple of days later it would be, 'No, they're right, this should be changed, I think we're going to change this.' So I couldn't really tell how much they really liked the idea of making the changes that were being suggested. Initially, I didn't like the idea of changing it at all. I wanted to know that they were going to go into the studio with Albini and they were going to walk out with a product from Albini. That's what I wanted to hear myself. I liked Albini for the same reasons that they did. I didn't like the idea of the record being messed with at all."

Cobain later talked about playing the record for a few weeks, trying to put his finger on what was wrong. "The first time I played it at home, I knew there was something wrong," he said. "I wasn't really interested in listening to it at all, and that usually doesn't happen. I got no emotion from it, I was just numb." Novoselic also talked frequently to Bailey. "We talked quite a bit about it," says Bailey. "I had a sound system in my restaurant, and after hours we would crank it up in there. We listened to it in different settings; we'd listen to it in the car, we'd listen to it when we were out dinging around. Krist was trying to get an idea of what people would hear. You're trying to put yourself in different situations when you're hearing the album." The consensus was that there were problems with the bass sound and the vocal mix.

Cobain eventually called Albini to share his concerns, as did Novoselic. "Kurt asked me about doing some remixes," Albini says. "I said, 'Alright, what songs are you talking about remixing?' Kurt named a few specifics, but then he said, 'But really, we'd like to redo it all.' He wanted to remix everything. Krist didn't think his bass guitar was well defined enough, there were certain songs where Kurt didn't think the vocals came out enough, but it was all subtleties. That was more evidence to me that this climate of fear had developed. They had made a great record, but the record label and all the other harpies in their life had managed to convince them that they had something to doubt.

"And I think Kurt was trying to articulate his position, which was that he felt uncomfortable that the people who were responsible for selling his record were uncomfortable with it," Albini continues. "He wanted to make himself confident. He wanted to make a record that he could slam down on the table and say, 'Listen, I know this is good, and I know your concerns about it are meaningless, so go with it.' And I don't think that he felt that he had that yet and that he wanted to redo stuff in hopes of getting there. My problem was that I feared a slippery slope. If we went back into the studio to remix it, it would have ended up being another situation like *Nevermind*, where it would have eventually been taken out of their hands. I knew if we got started on that path, it was going to be a replay of that."

In fact, *Nevermind* was originally going to be mixed by its producer, Butch Vig. But after mixing around six songs, the band's management and label suggested they bring in a fresh set of "ears." The band ultimately chose Andy Wallace, due to his previous work with Slayer. Yet they also seemed to have some ambivalence about the record's sound; when being interviewed for *Come As You Are*, just over a year after *Nevermind*'s release, Cobain claimed to be "embarrassed" by the record's production ("It's closer to a Motley Crüe record than it is a punk rock record"), Grohl felt the album "had a produced weirdness," and Novoselic called it "pretty hacked up....It's a really produced record." But ten years after *Nevermind*'s release, Novoselic insisted to an interviewer, "I know Kurt liked the way *Nevermind* sounded," though he still conceded the album was "kind of like a bubblegum record."

Vig's original mixes were rougher, lacking the glossy sheen of the final versions, but the material was also not as raw as the songs Nirvana recorded with Albini. And the band was more than willing to give Albini first shot at remixing. Albini appreciated the offer, but after listening to the album again ultimately declined. "I called Kurt back and said, 'Listen, if you guys want to remix some of this stuff, you have my blessing,'" he says. "'The subtleties in the recording that you're talking about—you can't change some of these things without fundamentally changing the presentation of the music.' I said that I just didn't feel like I could do any better. From a business standpoint, that was probably a bad idea, because I could have squeezed more money out of them. From a personal standpoint, I think that may have not set well with the band, that I wasn't willing to just say, 'Yeah, I'll do it all again.' But I know it was the right thing to say. I had a copy of that record before it was mastered. I saw that record at every stage of production. I knew that if it was manipulated beyond that point, some of that greatness was going to evaporate. And I just didn't want to be a party to it."

The matter may have ended there if not for the publication of Kot's article, "Record Label Finds Little Bliss in Nirvana's Latest," which appeared in the *Tribune* on April 19. "A source close to the band says Geffen executives are unhappy with the record's lack of commercial potential," read the article. "'They consider it unreleasable,' the source reported." The article also quoted Albini as saying, "Geffen and the band's management hate the record." A Geffen representative denied that this was the case, but admitted the record's release date had been pushed back due to a "hangup with mixing and mastering." And the band's manager,

John Silva, was given the last word; "If the band says the record's ready, then it's ready. But as of now, there is no Nirvana record to release."

After the story appeared, other media outlets began to pick it up, culminating in a full-page article by Jeff Giles that ran in *Newsweek*'s May 19 issue headlined "You Call This Nirvana?" The article implied the group was being pressured by their record company and management to remix the album, to keep the band from committing "commercial suicide," though it also featured a quote from Gersh, stating, "Nirvana has complete control over what they want to do with their record." The Nirvana camp quickly sent out a rebuttal letter-to-the-editor, which read in part, "Giles ridiculed our relationship with our label based on totally erroneous information. Geffen Records has supported our efforts all along in making this record." The text of the letter was also reprinted in a full-page ad in the May 22 edition of *Billboard* magazine, and the band also sent out a press release dated May 11, which began: "'There has been no pressure from our record label to change the tracks we did with [producer] Albini. We have 100% control of our music!' says Kurt Cobain of Nirvana."

The article also stated that Andy Wallace would be remixing the album. Wallace had initially been approached for the job, an indication that the group's objections to his work on *Nevermind* perhaps weren't as strong as they'd stated elsewhere. But when Wallace was unavailable, the band went with Scott Litt (best known for his work with R.E.M., and who had also been considered to remix *Nevermind*). And in the end, the band decided to only remix two tracks at the time, "Heart-Shaped Box" and "All Apologies." "I know for a while I felt like we shouldn't touch it as a point of principle," Novoselic later told writer Keith Cameron. "But that's not very rational. That stuff clouds your judgment." To another writer he explained that remixing the two songs would provide, "a gateway for people to buy the record, and then they'd put it on and have this aggressive wild sound, a true alternative record."

The remixes were done in May at Seattle's Bad Animals Studio, co-owned by Ann and Nancy Wilson of Heart. For "Heart-Shaped Box," Cobain also recorded another acoustic guitar part and added some backing vocals. The effect on the "Heart-Shaped Box" guitar solo was also removed, to Novoselic's relief. "Common sense prevailed," he says. "It was changed. Scott made the song nice."

The album was then sent off for mastering at the same studio where *Nevermind* had been mastered, and by the same person; Bob Ludwig, at Gateway Mastering in Portland, Maine. According to Azerrad, work done on the record was minimal, with the bass sharpened and vocals boosted. Unsurprisingly, Albini's ears heard it differently. "The dynamic range was narrowed, the stereo width was narrowed, there was a lot of mid-range boost EQ added, and the overall sound quality was softened," he said in 1996.

"And the bass response was compromised to make it sound more consistent on radio and home speakers. But the way I would describe it in non-technical terms is that they fucked it up. The end result, the record in the stores doesn't sound all that much like the record that was made."

It's an assessment he still agrees with. "Yes. You can fuck something up by trying too hard to make it good, by going through too many steps," he says. "If you're making a cake and you want it to be perfect, and you keep putting in little filigrees and touches of spices and ingredients, before long you have all of this stuff affecting itself. You wanted to make a great cake, but by continually twiddling with it, you ended up taking away some of its inherent quality."

Bailey also feels that "the album has a very compressed feel to it. A lot of that could be the guitar sound on it, because Kurt was using a different guitar pedal, and that's a big part of what I hear on an album, the guitar itself. The bass to me sounds very transparent.

"But I was fine with it," he adds. "When I actually heard some of the stuff they put in there, I did really like it. At the same time, too, you've had the first version for a period of time, and you've gotten used to it, so it then becomes almost difficult to listen to alterations because you're just becoming used to it. It's like listening to alternate tracks of Beatles songs. They'll just never sound the same to you because the one you've grown up with is 'the one,' whether it's better or not. I still think *In Utero*'s a phenomenal album."

Today Novoselic says, "I think in a lot of ways *In Utero* sounds amazing," but he also adds, "if I ever had the chance to remix it, I'd turn it up loud—I think the bass is kind of muddy." The matter also left Cobain with some mixed feelings. For all his complaints about *Nevermind*'s production, on October 25, he told writer David Fricke that "Pennyroyal Tea" was a track that "was not recorded right....That should have been recorded like *Nevermind*, because I know that's a strong song, a hit single," and the song would ultimately be remixed by Scott Litt a month later. As Azerrad astutely observed, "It seemed that Kurt was in love with the *idea* of the low-budget philosophy, but not its actuality" (emphasis Azerrad's). In his journal, Cobain fantasized about releasing the unmastered Albini version first, on vinyl, cassette, and 8-track tape to confound his audience; a CD release with the Ludwig-mastered version would then follow. But, contradictory to the end, he also told a journalist the final version of the album had "the sound we've had in our heads, that we've never been able to transfer [to a record]." He also paid Grohl a rare compliment about his drumming on the album, leaving a message on Grohl's answering machine that his work on *In Utero* was "awesome."

The unmastered Albini version of *In Utero* has since been widely bootlegged, allowing for ready comparison (and collectors have said the Albini mix is available on different vinyl pressings of the album). Play the two versions for the average listener, and the differences probably won't be immediately apparent. But a careful listen is more revealing; one then notices the harmony vocals on "Pennyroyal Tea" aren't as prominent on the original version, and are missing completely on "Heart-Shaped Box." The cello on "All Apologies" is also more pronounced on the final version, and the cymbals also have more of a shimmer throughout. The abrasiveness of Cobain's vocals on the harsher tracks like "Scentless Apprentice," "Milk It," and "Rape Me" is softened on the final version. In the end though, a preference for one version over the other may simply be a matter of taste.

By the time *In Utero* was released in September, the debates about whether Nirvana had "compromised" their sound were largely forgotten by the public. But Albini says the public spat had a "dramatic impact" on his business. "I almost went broke," he says. "I couldn't get arrested for about two years after I did that record. All the smaller bands that I worked with were sort of frightened off by the association with a band as popular as Nirvana, and all the bigger bands that I had worked with were frightened off by the political battle that Geffen waged with me." On the day *In Utero* reached #1 in the *Billboard* charts, he looked in his checkbook to find he had 50 cents left in his checking account.

But though Albini still maintains that "The ultimate presentation of that record I don't find flattering at all," he also insists that he has no lingering resentment about the *In Utero* experience. "I would hate it if the end perception of my talking about this was that I had hard feelings about the way that Nirvana treated me, because that's not the case at all," he says. "The band's situation was not enviable to me, but they made a great record. I was thrilled to be a part of it. By the time it was over, I was happy, I was proud, I was fond of those people, I had a lot of respect for them. There were things that have ameliorated that elation, or that have changed my remembrance slightly, but they're slight changes. I remember that record as a good one. I remember those people as good ones. I like and admire those guys.

"And the record that people have in their homes is the record that Nirvana wanted them to have," he concludes. "The band themselves made all the significant decisions about that record, so however convoluted or however less than ideal it might have been, that is still the record the band wanted people to hear. And I am for that."

Chapter 8
Artwork & Video

Much care and thought was also put into the creation of the visual imagery that accompanied *In Utero*'s release—the album cover, assorted singles, and the sole video, "Heart-Shaped Box," all of which drew heavily on Cobain's ideas.

The album's art director was Robert Fisher, who was then working in Geffen's art department, and had been involved with all Nirvana's projects since they signed to DGC. "When I heard that DGC had signed Nirvana, I was already a big fan and had seen them a few times, so I went 'Oh my God, let me work on it,'" he recalls. "So they let me. I don't think anyone really knew then what was going to happen with them. And they want someone that's into the band, into the music, to work on it, so it helps if you like the band."

Fisher went on to design covers for all the group's releases on DGC, and found that Cobain was often eager to make suggestions and pass on ideas. "I always thought his ideas were really cool," he says. "If you have a vision and you stick with it, then you've gotta get your props for that. And it makes it easier for me, because in designing for bands, it's really got to represent what the band is about and what they like. You get these bands that are like 'I don't care what's on the cover.' Well, that's kind of lame, because you should care, it's representing you. So the fact that Kurt cared and was interested, and we'd have talks about art and stuff, it was cool, I thought, that he cared what stuff looked like and that he had ideas. But he was never overbearing, like, 'Put this there and that there and do that.' He would just give me some loose odds and ends and say 'Do something with it.'"

The cover of the band's first album for DGC, *Nevermind*, featured a baby swimming underwater reaching out to grab a dollar bill on a fishhook, a perfect image of innocence on the verge of being corrupted. It had been widely acclaimed and continues to turn up on Best Album Cover lists, meaning there was pressure to come up with something equally strong for the much-anticipated second DGC album. "Because it's a high profile gig you want to do something amazing," Fisher agrees. "So there's always a lot of pressure to come up with good stuff."

And Cobain was very specific about the visual ideas he had for *In Utero*. For the front cover, he brought in a postcard of a Transparent Anatomical Mannikin (TAM), a see-through model of a woman. TAM had been designed by Richard Rush in 1968 as an educational tool for children; the model was wired so that different areas of the body could light up on cue. "Kurt had that image when we were doing *Nevermind*," says Fisher. "We were going to use it for a single, 'Lithium' or something. And for some reason it got scrapped and we went with something else, but that's the first time that I remember him bringing it to me." While *In Utero* would use a full body shot of TAM, an upper body shot of the model had appeared on the cover of the 1970 album *Music from the Body*, a soundtrack of a medical documentary, with music by Ron Geesin and Pink Floyd's Roger Waters.

The next step was securing the rights to the image. "We called around to try to get the rights to use it, and once they heard it was for Nirvana, then it was like, 'Alright, $80,000 and you can use it,'" says Fisher. "It was a really big thing in the company trying to figure out what to do. We even hired an illustrator to do a version of it that we could use without having to pay for the photo, changing it slightly. But they finally worked something out with the company that owned the rights to it." Wings were added to the woman as a final touch. "Kurt and I had a meeting, and we wanted to make it just a little bit more special," says Fisher. "And somehow we ended up having wings on it. I'm not sure if he asked for wings or if he asked me to try some different things and that's the one that he picked." The model was then placed against a pale yellow background, cracked like the surface of a desert. The image was actually a better reflection of the album's final title; after *I Hate Myself and I Want to Die* and *Verse Chorus Verse* had been considered and rejected, *In Utero* was the final choice. The TAM model wasn't pregnant, but its transparency nonetheless offered a "look within." The model also mirrored the Visible Man model used on the cover of Nirvana's "Sliver" single; the baby on the *Nevermind* cover helped complete the representation of the "family."

The front cover used the band's regular logo (set in Onyx, a condensed Bodoni typeface). The album's title had been punched out by Fisher on a Dymo label embosser. "I had one of those label makers in my office," he explains, "and so I did it and then I did a negative of it, and cut it out. As a designer, you're always looking for ways to experiment, trying different things and different ways of doing things; you're always looking for different angles. It's harder and harder these days to do something original. And then a year or two later I saw that label maker style as a typeface."

Fisher's use of label embosser type was unintentionally ironic. Designer Art Chantry, during his last stint as Art Director at the Seattle music publication *The Rocket*, had used a dysfunctional label embosser to design new column headings in the magazine. When the Seattle music scene exploded in the mainstream in 1992, the label embosser type style was quickly appropriated as a shorthand visual signifier of "alternative" culture, though cleaned up from its original presentation, with the letters properly aligned and all facing the right direction. *The Rocket* had been the first magazine to feature Nirvana on its cover, in 1989; now, four years later, a recycled element from the magazine again linked the two. Equally appropriately, the typeface replicating embossed label type is called "Recycle Reverse."

The CD's booklet featured the album's lyrics, perhaps reflecting a desire on Cobain's part to be taken seriously as a lyricist (no previous Nirvana album contained a lyric sheet, though the lyrics of *Nevermind* were later printed in the booklet for the "Lithium" single). "I feel embarrassed saying this, but I'd like to be recognized more as a songwriter," he told Gavin Edwards in 1993. "I don't pay attention to polls and charts, but I thumb through them once in a while and see, like, Eddie Vedder is nominated number-one songwriter and I'm not even listed." Also, in reviews of *Nevermind*, much had been made about how Cobain's singing style made it difficult to understand the words to his songs. Printing the lyrics on the sleeve would eliminate the confusion about what exactly Cobain was singing—though the meaning of the songs would be endlessly debated. Cobain also wrote descriptions of the songs in his journals, but according to Fisher, no liner notes were ever considered for the album.

The booklet also featured various photographs, most taken from live shows. The picture of Novoselic on television had been taken by Cobain's mother, Wendy O'Connor. "That came to me after the whole thing was practically done and they wanted to add it, last minute," says Fisher. "And I was like, 'Oh, I gotta fit this in somehow.'" There were also photographs of a burned-out Republican party campaign office that Fisher shot; "Kurt was about to leave town, and he had just heard that the building had burned down, so I ran down there on my lunch break to take some photos," he explains. There was also another illustration by Alex Grey of a pregnant woman without skin, revealing her muscles and bones. "That was an artist that Kurt was really into," say Fisher. "He had sent me a book of that guy's work and wanted to use one of the images from there." A small diagram of audio level settings was also added at the last minute.

The back cover featured a striking collage that had been designed by Cobain; a collection of human fetus models, body parts like arms and legs, and bones, lying among a bed of orchids and lilies, a "still life" he described as "Sex and woman and *In Utero* and vaginas and birth and death," an equally apt way to describe the themes of the album. The collage was photographed by Charles Peterson, whose pictures can be found on nearly all Nirvana releases. "I saw Kurt out somewhere, and he mentioned that he wanted me to shoot something for the cover," he recalls. "And I said, 'Yeah, let me know.' And I figured I'd be getting a call from the label or something. Then, one Sunday afternoon, Kurt calls me up, and is like, 'Hey, I want you to take that picture now.' And I'm like, 'Uh, you know, it's Sunday afternoon.' And he's like, 'No, you have to come over and do it now, I have 200 dollars worth of flowers here and they're gonna wilt.' And I'm like, 'Well, okay.' And I rummaged around for whatever film I had in the fridge, and went on over. It's so typical Kurt. It's a good thing I was home, let's put it that way."

Cobain had set up the collage on the floor of his Seattle home. "I actually thought it was pretty impressive that he had just done this whole thing on his living room floor," says Peterson, who arrived at the house in the early evening. "I'd asked him some questions about it before I came over, and he said it was about four feet by four feet—it was about the same size as a dining table, a four person dining table. So I thought, okay, I'm going to have to get up on something, and I recall bringing over a ladder. But it wasn't the easiest thing to photograph. And there was no way, on a Sunday afternoon, I could rent any particular equipment or anything for it; I just had to use what I owned." Peterson shot other photos during the session too; a shot of Love holding Frances Bean and looking at the collage appears in his book *Screaming Life*.

The film of the session was sent to Fisher, who "tweaked the color and made it that weird orange." The album's song titles were placed around the edge of the back cover, along with such symbols as a crescent moon, a bee, a triangle, and a corn doll, inspired by the book *The Woman's Dictionary of Symbols and Sacred Objects*, by Barbara Walker. "Kurt cut out all these little symbols and wanted to use them," says Fisher. "He said, 'Just put 'em around on the back somewhere,' and we hired an illustrator [Rodger Ferris] to re-illustrate them so that we could use them without copyright problems. Each of those little symbols meant something important to Kurt, that he was into" (the album's thank-yous also list "The Goddess Demeter"). In that sense, the *In Utero* packaging was not dissimilar to Cobain's *Journals*, which featured his artwork and clippings of images that interested him, as well as his writings.

The image on the CD itself was a picture of one of Frances Bean's nannies, Michael "Cali" DeWitt, in drag, taken from "a little Polaroid snapshot in the pile of stuff that Kurt liked, so I just put it on the disc and it was a go," says Fisher. Approval of the rest of the package was also readily forthcoming; "I just did the whole collage and the inside and Kurt was like, 'Okay, perfect.'"

Fisher also designed sleeves for *In Utero*'s three singles (none of which were released in America). "Heart-Shaped Box," released in August 1993, featured a photo by Cobain of a heart-shaped box in the middle of a bed of lilies and tinfoil. "Kurt gave me the picture, a little print from a one-hour photo place and said, 'Make something pretty,'" says Fisher. Fisher added a one-inch band at the bottom of heart-shaped beads pictured against a red background, with a drawing of the human heart on the left.

Cobain was less involved in the next two singles, though he did tell Fisher that for "All Apologies," released in

December 1993, he wanted "Something with seahorses." "And I went online and looked through books and found some seahorse pictures and just went from there," says Fisher. "He was really into the whole aspect that the males got to carry the young." Seahorses ended up on a t-shirt and a pin sold on Nirvana's last tours, and drawings of seahorses appear in Cobain's *Journals*.

Cobain had no input into the artwork for "Pennyroyal Tea," which was scheduled for release in April 1994; the track had been remixed by Scott Litt at Bad Animals on November 22, 1993. Playing off the song's title, the sleeve pictures a cup of tea on a table, next to an ashtray filled with cigarette butts and a rooster-shaped cream pitcher, with a few animal crackers scattered around. "We got it done and then I don't know that Kurt was around to approve it or not," says Fisher. "I think it might just have been shot over to management to approve or something." After Cobain's death, the single (which would have featured "I Hate Myself and Want to Die" and "Where Did You Sleep Last Night," the latter from *Unplugged*, as B-sides) was withdrawn and most copies were destroyed.

By that time, controversy had erupted over *In Utero*'s back cover. During the week of the album's US release, two major American discount chains, Wal-Mart and K-Mart, announced they were refusing to stock the album. The ostensible reason was said to be lack of customer demand— an odd claim to make about an album that entered the charts at #1—but the real reason was the retailers were afraid customers would find the fetus collage offensive.

As a result, the image was cropped so that it focused on the flowers and the fetuses were removed; a turtle that had originally been on the lower right corner was enlarged and moved to the left side. Even more bizarre was the insistence that the title of "Rape Me" also had to be changed. After briefly considering a change to the equally literal "Sexually Assault Me," the song was retitled "Waif Me." "Somewhere, someone was upset about it," says Fisher. "It was all just to move units in those stupid chain stores." As he wryly concludes, "We saved the nation."

The reworked edition was released on March 29, 1994. The band's true feelings about making the changes are disputed. Danny Goldberg, one of the band's managers, told writer Carrie Borzillo, "[Kurt] wanted very much for all of his fans to be able to get the records. He had complete control of that…There was no pressure." But Bill Bennett, then Geffen's General Manager, told Borzillo, "I think the record company really just pressured them. Left to their own devices, they never would have done it."

The creation of *In Utero*'s sole video, "Heart-Shaped Box," had its share of controversy as well, resulting in a lawsuit. Ideas for the video began coming together over the summer. In an interview, Cobain and Novoselic talked about the video with Jim DeRogatis, then describing it as "a spoof of *The Wizard of Oz* filmed in a technique approximating

Technicolor." Novoselic calls himself the "secretary" in the process. "Kurt goes, 'I want to do this video,'" he recalls. "And I said, 'Well, I got this new laptop. Why don't I bring it over, and I'll help you write it out.' So he's sitting there, and we wrote this two page treatment; he was dictating it and I would write it down."

The video was originally going to be directed by Kevin Kerslake, who had directed the group's previous four videos ("Come As You Are," "Lithium," "In Bloom," and "Sliver"). Carrie Borzillo's *Nirvana: The Day By Day Eyewitness Chronicle* provides the best chronology of what happened next. Kerslake prepared five treatments for the video between July 14 and August 12. But final arrangements to shoot the video never materialized. Instead, by the end of the month, Nirvana had engaged another director; Dutch filmmaker Anton Corbijn.

Corbijn had started his career as a rock photographer, moving from his native Holland to London in 1979 with the express goal of meeting and photographing the band Joy Division; one of his first shots of the group was a highly evocative black and white photograph of the band in the tunnel of a London tube station. He later moved into video, his first projects being clips for Palais Schaumburg ("Hockey") and Art of Noise ("Beatbox"). His first work with Nirvana was as a photographer; over the course of two days he shot photos for the November 1993 *Details* magazine cover story, and black and white promotional photos for DGC. "It was very enjoyable," he recalls. "And it was quite loose. In the studio of course I had a light, but for the rest I had no lights, and I had just one assistant and it was very simple, down to earth, and I think they quite liked that." Corbijn's black and white photos have a stark grittiness that is typical of his work; one of the *Details* shots captures Cobain in full decadent rock star mode, wearing a cowboy hat, sunglasses, a Jean Paul Gaultier-designed Lurex shirt tied high above his waist, and chipped nail polish.

Corbijn is not entirely certain how he ended up being approached to do the video. "I think Courtney told Kurt that I did videos, because she had lived in Liverpool for awhile, so she was aware of the Echo and the Bunnymen stuff I had done," he says. "Then Kurt asked if I could send him the Echo and the Bunnymen videos, which I did, and the next thing I knew, he and Krist sent me some faxes with drawings on it, and an idea about a video." A copy of the fax Cobain sent is reproduced in the booklet accompanying the DVD *The Work of Director Anton Corbijn*, with a sketch of the field that would be the primary set in the film.

Corbijn was surprised at the amount of detail in the unorthodox "treatment" he received. "It was all mapped out," he says. "It was incredibly precise. More precise than I'd ever had for a video. I loved it, but initially I was a bit taken aback that somebody came up with so many ideas, because generally my videos are my own ideas. So at first I thought well, maybe I shouldn't do it, if somebody else puts their own ideas in. But then I looked at it and I thought that actually it was pretty good. I was very amazed by somebody writing a song and having those ideas as precise as he did."

The video begins and ends with the band members in a hospital room, watching an old man lying in bed, hooked up to an IV with a fetus in the IV bag. But most of the action takes place in a surreal "outdoor" setting; a field of bright red poppies with a large cross standing in the middle, adjacent to a wood of creepy old trees (both elements in key scenes in *The Wizard of Oz*). In the first verse, the old man from the hospital, wearing a loincloth and Santa Claus hat, climbs onto the cross. The second verse introduces a little girl in a Ku Klux Klan outfit, who jumps up to try and catch the fetuses hanging from the trees, and similarly jumps up at the old man on the cross (now wearing a miter in place of the Santa hat); also seen is a fat woman wearing an oversize suit painted with organs of the human body. In the final cut, the band is not seen performing during the verses, only the choruses, playing beneath the trees, with Cobain's face leaping in and out of focus. The colors are bright enough to be almost lurid.

The Ku Klux Klan imagery had gone back to the "In Bloom" video, as detailed in *Come As You Are*; Cobain's *Journals* also feature a short storyboard for the video with the girl's KKK hat being blown off (an idea which was ultimately used in the "Heart-Shaped Box" video). Corbijn added some touches of his own, suggested using obviously fake butterflies and birds (Cobain had wanted to use real ones), and, inspired by *In Utero*'s cover, he came up with idea of the woman in the "organ suit," as "a mother earth kind of figure." He also added a ladder to the cross, "so the old man could climb onto it, which I thought was stranger and more dramatic," he says.

Corbijn also created the box the band is seen performing in during the final chorus, which has a large heart on top. "There's one very short shot where you see the whole box with the heart above it," he says. "That was my idea and they didn't like it. So very nicely, Krist during the shoot came up to me and said, 'Um, is it possible not to shoot from a distance 'cause we don't like it.' And later on, they actually did like it. And the little road through the field, there was no road initially, I made a little road through that." Cobain had originally wanted Beat author William Burroughs to play the old man, but Burroughs declined. Instead, they used a Los Angeles-based actor, "and it was very hard in LA to find an old man that looked old!" says Corbijn. He denies the rumor that the little girl was played by Cobain's half sister.

Cobain ended up wearing the same Jean Paul Gaultier-designed Lurex shirt he wore during the *Details* magazine shoot. "He was allowed to keep it, as long as he didn't use it for anything else," says Corbijn. "And of course it was in the video." Though seen in a black t-shirt in some shots, Novoselic wears a short-sleeved blue shirt in other shots that was given to him by Corbijn on the day of the shoot.

"Anton gave me the shirt off his back," Novoselic jokes. "Because he was thinking of the color scheme and he didn't like any of the shirts I brought. So he goes, 'You should wear a shirt like the one I have.' And somebody said, 'Well, why don't you give him yours?' And he goes 'OK,' and then he gave it to me."

The shoot was done at the end of summer and was largely uneventful. "Kurt was really great and one of the sweetest guys to work with," says Corbijn. "I really mean that. Anything he said was always positive criticism, and no negativity or anything." He also recalls Cobain being impressed with finished set; "I think he couldn't believe when he walked in that the set looked so much like what he had drawn on the piece of paper he'd sent me originally."

There was one disturbing moment involving the old man, though the band wasn't present. "He came off the cross and he fell down bleeding," says Corbijn. "He was standing, but suddenly he collapsed, and he had to be taken to the hospital. And it turned out he had cancer and he didn't know, and it opened up inside him, and there was all this blood coming out. It was very serious. And you can imagine, the ambulance people, when they arrived, seeing the set with the cross and everything, and there was this man lying there bleeding...I'm not sure whether they thought it was a snuff movie or something! We were all stunned for two or three hours; we couldn't work, it was pretty heavy. And he was a lovely man, a real character; he used to be a DJ on a jazz station. I visited him later in the hospital and Kurt gave me something to give to him. It was pretty heavy because of this song being about cancer; it was a bit spooky."

Cobain and Love came by while Corbijn was editing. In the first edit, Love urged Corbijn to use a single shot of Cobain singing the final verse. "Kurt looked amazing," he says, "and Courtney wanted to keep that shot till the very end. It was a very long take, but she persuaded Kurt to go with that." But Corbijn also did his own edit, which featured completely different shots during the final verse, showing the fat woman walking down the path and Cobain lying, eyes shut, in the field, smoke or mist rising around him. "They used Courtney's edit initially, and then they put mine out as well," says Corbijn. "And my edit became the video in the end." Corbijn's edit is the one you see on the *Anton Corbijn* DVD. The DVD also features an interview with Cobain, who stated, "That video has come closer to what I've seen in my mind, what I've envisioned, than any other video. I didn't think it would ever be possible to come that close." Novoselic agrees; "Anton did a beautiful job on that video."

But work on the video wasn't quite finished. Cobain had wanted to shoot in Technicolor, but was told the process was no longer used in the US. So Corbijn took a roundabout path to getting a similar effect, shooting in color, then transferring the film to black and white, then having the film hand-colored. "We wanted to have a sort of color that was hard to get," Corbijn explains. "I shot in color and then transferred to black and white because I felt that the black and white would have the right gradation for the colors to be hand-tinted. So we made a black and white version, and then we went to this place in San Diego and stayed there for a few weeks, and after every edit they hand-tinted the first frame, and once we'd approved it, it went across the border to Mexico, and there was a room with a hundred people in it that hand-tinted every frame till the next cut. It took a long time. But that's why the color looks so amazing."

Corbijn finds it interesting that though Fisher had to change *In Utero*'s back cover because of the fetus collage, no one made comments about the fetuses that can be seen in the video. "I mean, we have fetuses hanging off a tree, that's pretty heavy stuff, in most people's book," says Corbijn. "But I don't think anybody probably noticed these things because the colors are so lovely. I learned a lot from that—that people look a lot at the surface, not at the content. It really amazed me, I have to say." In fact there would be legal trouble over the video's imagery, though the issue was one of attribution; on March 9, 1994, Kerslake's attorneys filed a suit alleging copyright infringement. But the suit had no effect on the video's distribution, and was eventually settled out of court. The terms of the settlement were never disclosed.

Corbijn was later asked to direct the video for "Pennyroyal Tea." "But I decided not to do it," he says, "because I felt the 'Heart-Shaped Box' video was so good, I could never make a video that was as good or better. So I told Kurt that I felt that it was not right for me to do it, 'cause I didn't want to disappoint him. And then he said, 'Well then, I'll never make another video if you don't do it.' And he didn't." However, there are two treatments for a "Rape Me" video in Cobain's journals, with scenes set in a prison, footage of flowers and seahorses, and a man being prepared for a gynecological exam. And a 23-page video script of a proposed "Rape Me" video, with Jeffery Plansker listed as director, sold on eBay in January 2003 for $620.

On September 8, 1994, just under a year after its release, "Heart-Shaped Box" won two awards at the MTV Music Video Awards, for Best Alternative Video and Best Art Direction. "It should've won much more," in Corbijn's view. "It was only Best Alternative Video, which is a ridiculous thing, it should've won the Best Video full stop of that year."

Novoselic, Grohl, and second guitarist Pat Smear went onstage to accept the award for Best Alternative Video. "It'd be silly to say that it doesn't feel like there's something missing," said Grohl. "And I think about Kurt every day. And I'd like to thank everyone for paying attention to our band."

Chapter 9
In the End

Between *In Utero*'s completion and its release in September, Nirvana played three shows: April 9 at the Cow Palace in San Francisco (a benefit for the Tresnjevka Women's Group, who offered assistance to Bosnian rape victims); July 23 at the Roseland Ballroom in New York City; and August 6 at the King Theater in Seattle (a benefit for the Mia Zapata Investigative Fund; Zapata was the lead singer for Seattle band the Gits, and had been murdered the previous month), at which they played most of the *In Utero* songs. Anticipation about the album was heightened when *New Musical Express* writer Brian Willis was given an advance preview as the result of approaching Courtney Love for an interview after a show by her band Hole on July 1 at Seattle's Off Ramp club; he ended up being invited back to the Cobain/Love household where Cobain played him a tape of the album. Willis' cover story,

"Domicile on Cobain Street," appeared in *NME*'s July 24 issue and offered the first in-depth look at the record: "For Kurt, it represents a trip back to the womb and, listening to it, it's obvious he's done some deep soul-searching, with cathartic and, at times, manic results," he wrote.

The band had begun doing more official promotion for the album over the summer, agreeing to select media interviews. "Heart-Shaped Box" was released as a single August 23 with "Milk It" and "Marigold" as B-sides. September saw the release of the album. In the UK, *In Utero* was released on vinyl and cassette on September 13, and on CD September 14; in the US, a vinyl edition was released on September 14, with the CD following on September 21. The band made an appearance on "Saturday Night Live" on September 25, performing "Heart-Shaped Box" and "Rape Me." In October, the "Heart-Shaped Box" video was released, and the band began a US tour on October 18, with two new members: Pat Smear of the Germs, who played second guitar, and Lori Goldston of Seattle's Black Cat Orchestra on cello. On November 18, they recorded a performance for "MTV Unplugged"; of the fourteen-song set, three of the songs were from *In Utero*, while nearly half the set was comprised of covers.

No one had expected *In Utero* to match *Nevermind*'s sales; the record following a blockbuster album rarely matches its predecessor. Still, Cobain sounded somewhat defensive as he told Jim DeRogatis, "We're certain that we won't sell a quarter as much, and we're totally comfortable with that because we like this record so much. I wasn't half as proud of *Nevermind* as I am of this record. We intentionally made an aggressive record. I'm really proud of the fact that we introduced a different recording style, a different sound, and we're in a position where we're almost guaranteed a chance of it being played on the radio. They're at least going to try it for a while and see how it sticks. And just doing that is a satisfying accomplishment."

But in fact the album was both a commercial and a critical success. US sales in the first week were 180,000 copies, and *In Utero* entered the *Billboard* charts at #1; in the UK, the album also reached #1. "Heart-Shaped Box" also hit the top 10, reaching #1 on *Billboard*'s Modern Rock Tracks chart, and #5 in the UK. Many reviews were also positive, though some were mixed. "Nirvana have hit upon an almost perfect mix of inchoate rage and simple eloquently expressed fury," wrote *Melody Maker*, while *NME* was more circumspect: "*In Utero* is a profoundly confused record....A mess, but a bloody entertaining one." The *Los Angeles Times* called it a "brashly satisfying punk broadside. Catchy hooks are a lot fewer and farther-between here than on *Nevermind*, to be sure, but there's still a good amount of Buzzcocks-meets-Replacements flavor amid the thrash and din" while the *Washington Post* observed, "This is a different approach to the same tension between melody and crunch that made *Nevermind* exciting, and it works: Cobain's concerns may be increasingly hermetic, but *In Utero* is both musically and emotionally spacious." "*In Utero* is a lot of things," was *Rolling Stone*'s verdict. "Brilliant, corrosive, enraged and thoughtful, most of them all at once. But more than anything, it's a triumph of the will."

The reviews also confirmed that the success of *Nevermind* was not a fluke; Nirvana was now a solidly established act, a band it was assumed would be around for some time. In interviews, the band members might have expressed uncertainly about the group's longevity, but there was also a consensus that they would release further albums. Yet Cobain was also insistent that their music had to change, though he wavered in exactly how it might change. "I definitely don't want to write more songs like 'Pennyroyal Tea' and 'Rape Me,'" he told Michael Azerrad after the *In Utero* sessions. "I want to do more new wave, avant garde stuff with a lot of dynamics…I want to turn into the Butthole Surfers, basically." Conversely, he told David Fricke the band's next album would be "ethereal, acoustic," in the manner of R.E.M. Still, it was the desire to break away from a musical formula he now found "boring" that remained a consistent theme in Cobain's last interviews.

But though no one realized it, the band was in the process of winding down. "All Apologies" was released as a single in December, with "Rape Me" and "Moist Vagina," discreetly renamed "MV," as B-sides. Over the weekend of January 28-30, 1994, there was a final recording session at

Robert Lang Studios in Shoreline, Washington, that produced two jams and the song "You Know You're Right," the latter eventually released in 2002 (Grohl and Novoselic also recorded a number of other songs that remain unreleased). The band's last tour began with an appearance on the French TV show "Nulle Part Ailleurs" on February 4; it ended a month later, following a show at Munich's Terminal Einz on March 1, when the rest of the tour was cancelled due to Cobain's ill health. The final show featured eight of *In Utero*'s twleve songs; the last song the band performed that night was "Heart-Shaped Box." On March 4, while in Rome, Cobain was rushed to the hospital after overdosing on a near-lethal combination of champagne and the prescription sleeping drug rohypnol. On April 8, Cobain was found dead in his Seattle home of a self-inflected gun-shot wound. Three days later, *In Utero* was certified double platinum in the US.

Cobain's sudden, shocking, and tragic demise immortalized him as a rock 'n' roll martyr, the "reluctant icon of a generation" as he was quickly painted in the media. But this view has also at times threatened to overshadow his artistic legacy. Cobain himself sometimes publicly disparaged his own legacy; asked by Azerrad if he felt Nirvana would have any lasting influence, he responded "Fuck no." But the care he invested in every aspect of his recordings suggests he felt otherwise, as do his statements about wanting to further develop his music.

In fact, Nirvana's music had developed over the years, as is evident by playing *Bleach*, *Nevermind*, and *In Utero* side by side. No one can say for certain what Nirvana's next work would have sounded like. But despite the pressure of having to make a follow-up to an internationally acclaimed multi-million-seller in the unexpected glare of the spotlight, *In Utero* depicts a band at the top of their game and still in the process of evolving, still interested in experimenting with new musical and lyrical ideas, still caught up in the joy and intensity of artistic creation. It's a culmination of everything the band had done to date, as well as a tantalizing indication of what they might have gone on to do in the future.

Most importantly, it stands as a first-rate album in its own right. "That's my favorite Nirvana record," says Krist Novoselic. "Because with all the stuff that was going on, what we did was we got together and we started rehearsing and we left everything at the door and we started playing some great music. And we put a record together. And that's all that really mattered."

Bibliography

<u>Articles:</u>

Cameron, Keith. "This Is Pop," *Mojo*, May 2001.

Edwards, Gavin. "Heaven Can Wait," *Details*, November 1993.

DeRogatis, Jim. "Womb Service," *Guitar World*, October 2003.

———. "Complications: The Difficult Birth of *In Utero*," *Guitar World*, October 2003.

Doyle, Tom. "No Pain, No Gain," *Q*, September 2005.

Fricke, David. "Sleepless in Seattle," *Rolling Stone*, September 16, 1993.

———. "Kurt Cobain: The *Rolling Stone* Interview," *Rolling Stone*, January 27, 1994.

Gaar, Gillian G. "Verse Chorus Verse: The Recording History of Nirvana," *Goldmine*, February 14, 1997.

———. "Nirvana: The Lost Tapes," *Mojo*, May 2004.

———. "Collecting Nirvana," *Discoveries*, September 2004.

———. "Good Riffs. Good Drumming. Great Screaming!" *Mojo*, January 2005.

———. "Nirvana: What's Left in the Vaults?" *Goldmine*, January 20, 2006.

Giles, Jeff. "You Call This Nirvana?" *Newsweek*, May 19, 1993.

Jenkins, Mark. "Pop Recordings," *The Washington Post*, September 19, 1993.

Kot, Greg. "Record Label Finds Little Bliss in Nirvana's Latest," *Chicago Tribune*, April 19, 1993.

Mitchell, Ben. "A Life Less Ordinary," *Q*, December 2005.

Mulvey, John. "Band of Fallopian Glory," *New Musical Express*, September 4, 1993.

O'Connell, Sharon. "Womb at the Top," *Melody Maker*, September 4, 1993.

Orshoski, Wes. "Dave Grohl: Honor Roll," *Harp*, October 2005.

Romance, Laurence. "I Want to Go Solo Like Johnny Cash: The Unpublished Interview," *Uncut Legends #2: Kurt Cobain*, March 2004.

Savage, Jon. "Sounds Dirty: The Truth About Nirvana," *The Observer*, August 15, 1993.

Scaggs, Austin. "On an Honor Roll," *Rolling Stone*, July 28, 2005.

Silva, John. "Letter of Appeal," *BigO*, November 1993.

Stud Brothers, The. "Dark Side of the Womb" (Parts 1 and 2), *Melody Maker*, August 21 & 28, 1993.

Sutcliffe, Phil. "King of Pain," *Q*, October 1993.

Thompson, Dave. "The Boys Are Back in Town," *Alternative Press*, October 1993.

True, Everett. "In My Head I'm So Ugly," *Melody Maker*, July 18, 1992.

———. "Nirvana: Crucified By Success?" *Melody Maker*, July 25, 1992.

Willis, Brian. "Domicile on Cobain Street," *New Musical Express*, July 24, 1993.

Willman, Chris. "Nirvana's Brash Punk With Spunk," *Los Angeles Times*, September 19, 1993.

Books:

Arnold, William. *Shadowland*. New York: Jove/HBJ, 1979.

Azerrad, Michael. *Come As You Are: The Story of Nirvana*. New York: Main Street Books, 1994.

Borzillo, Carrie. *Nirvana: The Day By Day Eyewitness Chronicle*. New York: Thunder's Mouth Press, 2000.

Cobain, Kurt. *Journals*. New York: Riverhead Books, 2002.

Peterson, Charles. *Screaming Life: A Chronicle of the Seattle Music Scene*. San Francisco: HarperCollins West, 1995.

Rocco, John (editor). *The Nirvana Companion*. New York: Schirmer Books, 1998.

Websites:

allmusic.com

livenirvana.com

nirvanaguide.com

roadsideamerica.com

Other:

Entertain Us: The Story of Nirvana. BBC Radio 1 broadcast, April 5, 1999.

"Nirvana's Kurt Cobain Debunks Rumors of Geffen Interference with New Album." Press release, Geffen Records, May 11, 1993.

"Nirvana: Past Present and Future." MTV broadcast, February 7, 1994.

The Work of Director Anton Corbijn. DVD, Director's Label/Palm Pictures, 2005.

Also available in the series

ALSO AVAILABLE IN THE SERIES